The Work Addiction Workbook

Information, Assessments, and Tools for Managing Life with a Behavioral Addiction

Ester R.A. Leutenberg and John J. Liptak, EdD

Whole Person Associates
Mental Health & Wellness Publishers
Duluth, Minnesota

Whole Person Associates

101 West 2nd Street, Suite 203
Duluth, MN 55802-5004

800-247-6789

Books@WholePerson.com
WholePerson.com

The Work Addiction Workbook

Editorial Director: Jack Kosmach
Art Director: Mathew Pawlak
Cover Design: Adam Sippola
Editor: Peg Johnson

Library of Congress Control Number: 2022939810
ISBN:978-1-57025-366-9

From the co-authors, Ester and John,
Our gratitude, thanks, and appreciation
to the following professionals:

Editorial Directors – Jack Kosmach and Peg Johnson

Editor and Lifelong Teacher – Eileen Regen, MEd, CIE

Reviewer – Niki Tilicki, MA Ed

Proofreader – Jay Leutenberg, CASA

Art Director – Mathew Pawlak

A Special Thank You
to
Whole Person Associates

for their interest in mental health issues.

Free PDF Download Available

To access your free PDF download of the assessment tools
and all of the reproducible activities in this workbook, go to:
https://WholePerson.com/store/TheWorkAddictionWorkbook9810.html

Understanding Behavioral Addictions

There are many types of addictions. The behavioral addictions that are heard about most are substance abuse addictions. However, a behavioral addiction can be the same as a physical dependence on a substance.

> ...it is the compulsive nature of the behavior that is often indicative of a behavioral addiction, or process addiction, in an individual. The compulsion to continually engage in an activity or behavior despite the negative impact on the person's ability to remain mentally and physically healthy and functional in the home and community defines behavioral addiction. The person may find the behavior rewarding psychologically or get a "high" while engaged in the activity but may later feel guilt, remorse, or even be overwhelmed by the consequences of that continued choice. Unfortunately, as is common for all who struggle with addiction, people living with behavioral addiction cannot to stop engaging in the behavior for any length of time without treatment and intervention.

~ American Addiction Centers (2019)

People are increasingly experiencing non-substance behavioral addictions and diminished control over the behavior. Behavioral addictions are no longer categorized as impulse disorders. Behavioral addictions are now viewed as true addictions, much like substance abuse.

The National Institute of Health (2010) states:

> Growing evidence suggests that behavioral addictions resemble substance addictions in many domains, including natural history, phenomenology, tolerance, comorbidity, overlapping genetic contribution, neurobiological mechanisms, and response to treatment.

~ Grant et al. 2010

The concept of addiction, for years adopted solely to indicate the use of psychotropic substances, is now being applied to describe a heterogeneous group of syndromes known as "behavioral addictions," "no-drug addictions," or "new addictions." Prevalence rates for such conditions, taken as a whole, are amongst the highest registered for mental disorders with social, cultural, and economic implications. Individual forms of behavioral addictions are linked by a series of psychopathological features that include repetitive, persistent, and dysfunctional behaviors, loss of control over behavior despite the negative repercussions of the latter, compulsion to satisfy the need to implement the behavior, initial well-being produced by the behavior, craving, onset of tolerance, abstinence and, ultimately, a progressive, significant impairment of overall individual functioning.

Why Are They Called Behavioral Addictions?

Behavioral addictions constitute any maladaptive pattern of excessive behavior that manifests in physiological, psychological, and cognitive symptoms such as the following:

- **Continuance:** continuing the behavior despite knowing that this activity is creating or exacerbating physical, psychological, or interpersonal problems.

- **Intention effects:** inability to stick to one's routine, as evidenced by exceeding the amount of time devoted to the behavior or consistently going beyond the intended amount.

- **Lack of control:** unsuccessful attempts to reduce the level of the behavior or cease it for a certain period of time.

- **Reduction in activities:** as a direct result of the behavior, social, familial, occupational, or recreational activities occur less often or are stopped.

- **Time:** a great deal of time is spent preparing for, engaging in, and recovering from the behavior.

- **Tolerance:** increasing the amount of the behavior to feel the desired effect, be it a "buzz" or a sense of accomplishment.

- **Withdrawal:** in the absence of the behavior, the person experiences adverse effects such as anxiety, irritability, restlessness, and sleep problems.

Addiction to Work

Work addiction is one of the most common behavioral addictions. Behavioral addiction is an addiction to specific behaviors that alter a person's mood and brain chemistry. The term addiction encompasses any recurring compulsion or obsession by a person despite negative life and career consequences. It is punctuated by an inability to slow or stop the behavior and end it permanently. The addictive behavior becomes a significant problem because there is no work-life balance, and boundaries are weak. When people are addicted to the work in which they are engaged, they are considered to have a work addiction. Work addiction, commonly referred to as workaholism, is an actual mental health condition. Like any other addiction, work addiction occurs when people cannot stop overworking.

People develop work addiction for a variety of reasons:
- A compulsive need to achieve higher status at work.
- A desire to be successful at a job.
- To escape emotional stress.
- An excuse to be away from home.
- A need to be perfect in the work one does.
- The necessity to make more money.

Like someone with a substance addiction, people with a work addiction achieve a "high" from working. This high then leads them to keep repeating the work-related behavior to continue attaining an additional feeling of buzz, and so on. People with a work addiction may be unable to stop the behavior despite the negative ways it may affect their personal life, physical well-being, or mental health. Unlike people with a substance abuse addiction, people addicted to work usually have difficulty knowing they have a problem. Workaholism is sometimes considered a positive, and, in those cases, people are often admired for their behavior and believed to be conscientious workers.

WORK ADDICTION IN THE DSM-5

Although absent from the present diagnostic guidelines, such as the World Health Organization (2018) International Classification of Diseases (ICD) and the American Psychiatric Association's (2018) Diagnostic and Statistical Manual of Mental Disorders (DSM-5), experts have recognized that work may have an addiction potential and that some forms of obsessive working represent an addicted behavior.

The latest edition of the Diagnostic and Statistical Manual of Mental Disorders (DSM-5) reconceptualized addictive behavior to include behavioral addictions akin to more traditional drug addictions. Two profound changes were made: Gambling Disorder (formerly pathological gambling) was reclassified as a behavioral addiction rather than a disorder of impulse control, and Internet Gaming Disorder was introduced into Section 3 of the DSM-5. However, at present, although these changes represent a substantial recognition of behavioral addictions in general, workaholism has not yet been formally included in the DSM.

Workaholism has been defined by Andreassen, Hedland, and Pallesen (2014) as "being overly concerned about work, driven by an uncontrollable work motivation, and investing so much time and effort to work that it impairs other important life areas" (p. 8). Research into workaholism has greatly expanded over the past few decades, and concerns have been raised regarding the problem of workaholism. There has been increased interest in workaholism becoming a mental health disorder, especially since modern technology (laptops, tablets, smartphones) has blurred the natural lines between home and the workplace.

The constant preoccupation with work can be a behavioral addiction that can usually be effectively treated using a range of cognitive and behavioral therapies.

Potential Symptoms of Work Addiction

A person becomes increasingly at risk of work addiction as the intensity of time spent working and thinking about work escalates. Many people who are addicted to work find that they cannot stop their obsessive work habits, take work home on the evenings and weekends, and refuse to take vacations unless they are working. Their addiction to work becomes obvious when work-related behaviors disrupt various aspects of their lives, including relationships, family, friendships, and workplace performance. The symptoms of work addiction can be physical, emotional, and social.

People with a work addiction may experience that they ...
- Neglect family.
- Cannot "let go" and delegate work.
- Have no time to spend with friends.
- Develop problems in their social life.
- Use work to maintain their self-worth.
- Spend more time at work than they intended.
- Find themselves becoming angry and irritated easily.
- Become depressed if they are prevented from working.
- Increase time at work without an increase in productivity.
- Feel unhappy despite their financial success.
- Experience withdrawal symptoms if they are not working.
- Ignore suggestions or requests from others to cut down on work.
- Use work to cope with, escape, or numb feelings.
- Think obsessively about how they can free up more time for work.
- Prioritize work phone calls over family members' phone calls.
- Suffer deteriorating physical health due to an excessive work schedule.
- Develop a 'high' at work and need to work more to get the same effects.
- Have health problems resulting from work-related stress or overwork.
- Are unable to enjoy the fruits of their labor because of workaholic issues.
- Have difficulty relaxing and disengaging from work, even when on vacation.
- Attempt to reduce feelings of guilt, depression, anxiety, or hopelessness because of what they perceive as their inadequate contribution to family finances.
- Feel out of control or powerless when setting work limits, leaving the workplace for legitimate reasons during the workday, or quitting work for the day.
- Promise to spend more time at home or engage in recreation and do not follow through.
- Believe that their family does not care that they are respected and admired in their company or industry.
- Continue to "push their limits" despite warnings from their doctor, psychologist, family member, colleague, or supervisor.
- Find that relationship problems result from overwork or preoccupation with work.
- Are unsuccessful in their attempts to cut down or stop overworking, over-committing, and staying at the office.
- Break promises to themselves, their family, or their friends regarding work time, travel schedules, and other employment-related activities.
- Believe their work patterns are their fun times rather than family, sports, museums, or other relaxing activities.

Those with a mild work addiction may exhibit between four and five of these behaviors. In contrast, those with a moderately severe work addiction may exhibit six to seven of these behaviors. People who suffer from a severe work addiction will often exhibit most or all of the above behaviors.

Levels of Work Addiction

People who are addicted to work go through various levels of addiction. They need to monitor their work-related behaviors to ensure they do not move from hard-working employees who love the work to full-blown work addicts. As with any addiction, catching it in its earlier stages proves to be more successful in dealing with withdrawal effects.

Hard Worker: A hard worker is available for family members, co-workers, and friends, and maintains a healthy balance between work and personal responsibility. When overextending to meet an important deadline or an emergency, the hard worker tries to have some days off to restore depleted resources.

Early Stage: In this stage of work addiction, workers tend to be constantly busy and take on more than they can realistically do. They do not like to say NO! They put in a lot of extra hours, whether paid for overtime or not and cannot seem to find ways to take days off. They will sometimes relinquish a few of their vacation days.

Middle Stage: At this stage of work addiction, workers begin to distance themselves from personal relationships and responsibilities. When at home, they are distracted and remain at work emotionally. They often wish they could be at work rather than at home. Physical exhaustion often takes a toll. They perseverate about work and cannot unwind enough to fall asleep. They may feel tired all the time. They may see weight changes.

Late Stage: Those in the late stage of work addiction now tend to exhibit more serious physical and emotional symptoms like chronic headaches, elevated blood pressure, stomach ulcers, increased risk of stroke, etc. They experience and feel extreme fatigue. They work all the time and do not take any days off. Their relationships with loved ones may suffer.

Psychological Issues of Work Addiction

People who are addicted to work have psychological issues that drive their need to work:

- **Preoccupation with Work:** They overwork, and when not at work, they obsess about it to the point that their lives swing out of balance, negatively affecting their health and relationships.

- **Low Self-Esteem**: They are overly concerned with their image and believe overworking earns them the admiration of others. Often, they think bringing in more money can make up for the time not spent at home.

- **Control Issues:** They work to cope with life's uncertainties and try to gain control over the things in their life that seem uncontrollable.

- **Approval Seeking:** Their identity is their work, and it justifies their existence. It becomes a means of gaining approval from people at work, home, friends, and acquaintances.

- **Authority Issues:** They are prone to submitting to authority figures in a search for approval, even if it means surrendering or lowering themselves in ways they ordinarily would not.

- **Perfectionism:** They make unreasonable demands upon themselves. These include expectations for those around them at work and in personal relationships.

- **Escapism:** They use work to escape managing their emotions and feelings.

- **Lying:** They lie to themselves and others about their work habits. They may also lie about past successes and failures, exaggerating the former and minimizing or falsifying the latter.

Using This Workbook

The Work Addiction Workbook provides helping professionals with cognitive and behavioral assessments, tools, and exercises that can be utilized to treat the root causes of work addiction and to help people identify and change negative, unhealthy thoughts and behaviors that may have led to work addiction.

The activities in this workbook can assist participants in identifying their work addiction triggers and teach them ways to overcome and manage those triggers. This workbook can help participants to achieve the following:

- Become aware and recognize that they are experiencing an addiction problem.

- Realize and reflect on the behaviors that were part of, and arose from, the addiction.

- Build self-esteem in positive aspects of their personality and non-work-related skills.

- Recognize the triggers of preoccupation with various aspects of working behavior.

- Develop greater self-acceptance and the ability to change ineffective behaviors.

- Understand recurring patterns that indicate an addiction to work.

- Learn ways to live a new life without the need to obsess about working.

The Work Addiction Workbook is a practical tool for teachers, counselors, and helping professionals in their work with people suffering from work addictions. Depending on the person's role using this workbook and the specific group or individual needs, the modules can be used individually or as part of an integrated curriculum. The facilitator can administer an activity with a group or individual or use multiple assessments in a workshop.

Confidentiality When Completing Activity Handouts

Participants will see the words **USE NAME CODES** on some of the activities in the modules. Instruct participants that when writing or speaking about anyone, they need to **USE NAME CODES** for people to preserve privacy and anonymity. These codes will allow participants to explore their feelings without hurting anyone's feelings or fearing gossip, harm, or retribution. For example, a friend named **Jason,** who **P**lays **V**olleyball **W**ell, might be assigned a name code of **PVW** for a particular exercise. To protect others' identities, participants will <u>not</u> use people's actual names or initials, only **NAME CODES.**

© 2023 WHOLE PERSON ASSOCIATES, 101 WEST 2ND STREET, SUITE 203, DULUTH MN 55802 • 800-247-6789 • WHOLEPERSON.COM

The Five Modules

This workbook contains five modules of activity-based handouts that will help participants learn more about themselves and their addiction to work. These modules serve as avenues for self-reflection and group experiences revolving around topics of importance in the participants' lives.

The activities in this workbook are user-friendly and varied to provide a comprehensive way of analyzing, strengthening, and developing characteristics, skills, and attitudes for overcoming an addiction to work.

The activities and handouts in this workbook are reproducible. Minor revisions to suite client or group needs are permitted, but the copyright statement must be retained.

Module 1: Psychological Need
This module helps participants become aware of and explore the psychological issues that drive them to need to work all the time. They examine how their obsession with work causes problems, including damaged relationships, health problems, and an inability to slow down and enjoy life outside of work. They learn methods to manage psychological needs driving them to overwork, such as low self-esteem, work as a coping mechanism, and approval-seeking behavior.

Module 2: My Work Patterns
This module helps participants explore and recognize the patterns that lead to a work-related problem. They examine how they live in denial and do not see how their overworking patterns affect them and the people in their lives. They endeavor to become aware of their overworking patterns and how these patterns are often the starting point of their recovery.

Module 3: I Have a Problem
This module helps participants examine how their work addiction is a maladaptive pattern of excessive behavior that manifests in physiological, psychological, and cognitive symptoms. Participants discuss how their addiction encompasses the same symptoms as someone addicted to a substance. Exercises are included to help them examine the extent of their work addiction.

Module 4: Maintain Wellness
This module helps participants realize they are at risk of burning out because of their work addiction unless they maintain a sense of wellness. They examine their emotional, physical, and mental exhaustion caused by excessive and prolonged work stress. Activities are included to help them feel less overwhelmed and emotionally drained and to build the ability to cope with the stress of life.

Module 5: Work-Life Balance
This module helps participants overcome an imbalance between their work and other life roles, such as their personal and family life. They will examine ways to develop a better work-life balance to split their time and energy between work and other vital aspects of life. They will learn tools and techniques for balancing work and life.

Different Types of Activity Handouts Included in This Workbook

A variety of materials are included in this reproducible workbook:

- **Action Plans** that assist participants in meeting the goals and objectives of treatment.

- **Assessments** that allow participants to explore their behavior. Assessments can be used to measure progress before and after working on the topic.

- **Drawing and Doodling** to unleash the power of the right side of the brain.

- **Educational Pages** that provide insights and tips related to the topic.

- **Group Activities** to encourage collaboration among participants.

- **Journaling activities** can help participants clarify their thoughts and feelings, thus gaining helpful self-knowledge.

- **Quotation Pages** allow participants to reflect on many powerful quotes and determine how they may apply them to their lives.

- **Tables** that require participants to reflect on their lives in the past, understand themselves in the present, and respond more effectively in the future.

References

American Addiction Centers (2019). Behavioral Addictions. Americanaddictioncenters.org.

American Psychiatric Association (2018). Diagnostic and Statistical Manual of Mental Disorders (DSM–5) https://www.psychiatry.org/Psychiatrists/Practice/DSM

Andreassen CS, Hetland J, Pallesen S. (2014). Psychometric assessment of workaholism measures. *Journal of Managerial Psychology, 29, 7–24.*

National Institute of Health (2010). Introduction to Behavioral Addictions. www.ncbi.nlm.nih.gov/search

World Health Organization (2018). International Classification of Diseases (ICD) Information Sheet. www.who.int/home

Table of Contents

(Continued on page xiv)

Table of Contents

(Continued on page xv)

    © 2023 WHOLE PERSON ASSOCIATES, 101 WEST 2ND STREET, SUITE 203, DULUTH MN 55802 • 800-247-6789 • WHOLEPERSON.COM

Table of Contents

Psychological Need

Name _____

Date _____

Psychological Need Assessment
Introduction and Directions

Working a lot can seem like a noble endeavor. However, people addicted to work obsessively engage in the behavior and cannot stop even though it begins to affect their health and well-being. They crave work and will obsessively work until they are unable to continue.

It is vital to explore the psychological issues that drive you to NEED to work all the time. This obsession with work causes many problems, including damaged relationships, health problems, and an inability to slow down, relax, and enjoy life outside work.

The following assessment contains 20 statements that describe psychological issues people face when they are addicted to work. Read each of the statements and decide whether it describes you. If it describes you, place a checkmark in the box in front of the statement. If it does not describe you, leave the box in front of the statement empty.

In the following example, the first statement is descriptive of the person completing the assessment, but the second is not:

When it comes to working:

☑ My identity is in my work, and work justifies my existence.

☐ Work is a means of gaining approval from others.

This is not a test. Since there are no right or wrong answers, do not spend too much time thinking about your answers. Be sure to respond to every statement. The purpose of this assessment is for YOU to learn more about YOU and your work habits.

BE HONEST!

If you choose, no one else needs to see the results.

(Turn to the next page and begin.)

Psychological Need Assessment

Name _____ Date _____

This will only be accurate if you respond honestly. No one else needs to see this if you choose.

When it comes to working:

☐ My identity is in my work, and work justifies my existence.

☐ Work is a means of gaining approval from others.

☐ I'm overly concerned with my professional image.

☐ I believe that overworking earns me the admiration of significant others in my life.

☐ I use work to cope with the uncertainties of my life.

☐ I try to gain a measure of control over the uncontrollable aspects of my life.

☐ I am prone to surrendering to authority figures in my search for approval.

☐ I often try to please supervisors to get more work.

☐ I tend to make unreasonable, perfectionistic work demands on myself.

☐ At work and in my relationships, I often expect others to be perfect.

☐ I work in order to escape dealing with life issues.

☐ I use work as an excuse when I am feeling overwhelming emotions.

☐ I tend to overwork a lot of the time.

☐ I am preoccupied with work.

☐ When not at work I obsess about working.

☐ I feel like my life is becoming out of balance.

☐ I am experiencing problems with my health.

☐ I feel like work is interfering with my relationships.

☐ I have begun to lie to myself and others about my work behaviors.

☐ I exaggerate my successes and minimize or falsify my failures.

TOTAL Checked Answers = _____

Go to the next page for scoring assessment results, profile interpretation, and individual description.

Psychological Need Assessment

Scoring Directions and Profile Interpretations

The assessment you just completed measures your psychological need to work. Count the number of items you checked. Put that total on the line marked TOTAL on the assessment at the bottom of the page. Then, transfer your total to the space below:

Psychological Need TOTAL = _____

Assessment Profile Interpretation

By checking even ONE statement, you might be experiencing problems in your life due to an addiction to work. The more items you checked, the greater your risk of experiencing issues because of your work addiction.

The HIGHER your score on the Psychological Need Assessment, the more of a work addiction you are experiencing. Place an X on the continuum below for your score.

0 = Low	**10 = Moderate**	**20 = High**

Were you honest when completing the assessment? Is your score valid?

_____

_____

What is your reaction to your score?

_____

_____

Do you feel you need to do something about your psychological work issues?

_____

_____

Reforming Your Identity

An identity is made up of much more than work. When people are addicted to work, their identity lies primarily in their work. It becomes their primary reason for being. Their entire identity. It's why they get up in the morning.

In the spaces below, list your other non-work life roles (student, volunteer, friend, parent, partner, lover, school board member, religious student, etc.). ***Then list how you can integrate them into your identity and how this will add meaning to your life.***

My Life Roles	How I Can Integrate It Into My Identity	How This Will Add Meaning to My Life
Example: Parent	I want to start spending more time with my children and working less.	I'll feel more self-respect and integrity as a parent.

Caution! When people experience stress, many rely solely on their work identity as a compensatory method of feeling alive and adding meaning to life. Identity formation is discovering who you are outside of work and finding ways to integrate these roles to add value and meaning to your life.

Approval-Seeking Behavior

People addicted to work need approval from work supervisors. Whose approval do you need?

On the line under each symptom of approval-seeking behavior, place an X on the continuum based on much you relate to the statement. Write why you rated yourself that way on the dotted line below each one. BE HONEST!

I soften or change my opinion if the person disapproves.

0 (Not Like Me)   5 (Somewhat Like Me)   10 (Much Like Me)

I pay the person compliments I don't mean to gain approval.

0 (Not Like Me)   5 (Somewhat Like Me)   10 (Much Like Me)

I feel insulted if the person disagrees with me.

0 (Not Like Me)   5 (Somewhat Like Me)   10 (Much Like Me)

Even if I don't agree with the person, I will concur.

0 (Not Like Me)   5 (Somewhat Like Me)   10 (Much Like Me)

I take on unwanted work to avoid saying no to the person.

0 (Not Like Me)   5 (Somewhat Like Me)   10 (Much Like Me)

I don't complain even when the person takes advantage of me.

0 (Not Like Me)   5 (Somewhat Like Me)   10 (Much Like Me)

HIGHER SCORES (Much Like Me) on the above statements indicate that you desperately need the approval of someone at work, no matter what it costs you!

MEDIUM SCORES (Somewhat Like Me) other than a 0 indicate some work issues.

LOWER SCORES (Not Like Me) suggest that you are not experiencing too many signs of a work problem.

Self-Esteem

People with a work addiction seek self-esteem through work. They are often overly concerned with their professional image and don't feel good about the other aspects of their lives.

In the spaces below, explore other talents, personality characteristics, and energy you have to offer.

Other Aspects of My Life	What I Have to Offer
Example: Relationships	*I am social. I love meeting new people, joining a book club, inviting neighbors to a cookout, and accepting social invitations.*
Relationships	
Friends	
Community Activities/Volunteering	
Spiritual Activities	
Spare-Time Activites	
Other	

To establish true self-esteem, we must concentrate on our successes
and forget about the failures and the negatives in our lives.
~ Denis Waitley

Admiration (Page 1)

Admiration is defined as respect or approval of another.

Work addicts believe that overworking earns them the admiration of significant others in their life. In the circles below, list how people admire you for your hard work. List the person and why you believe they admire you. **USE NAME CODES.**

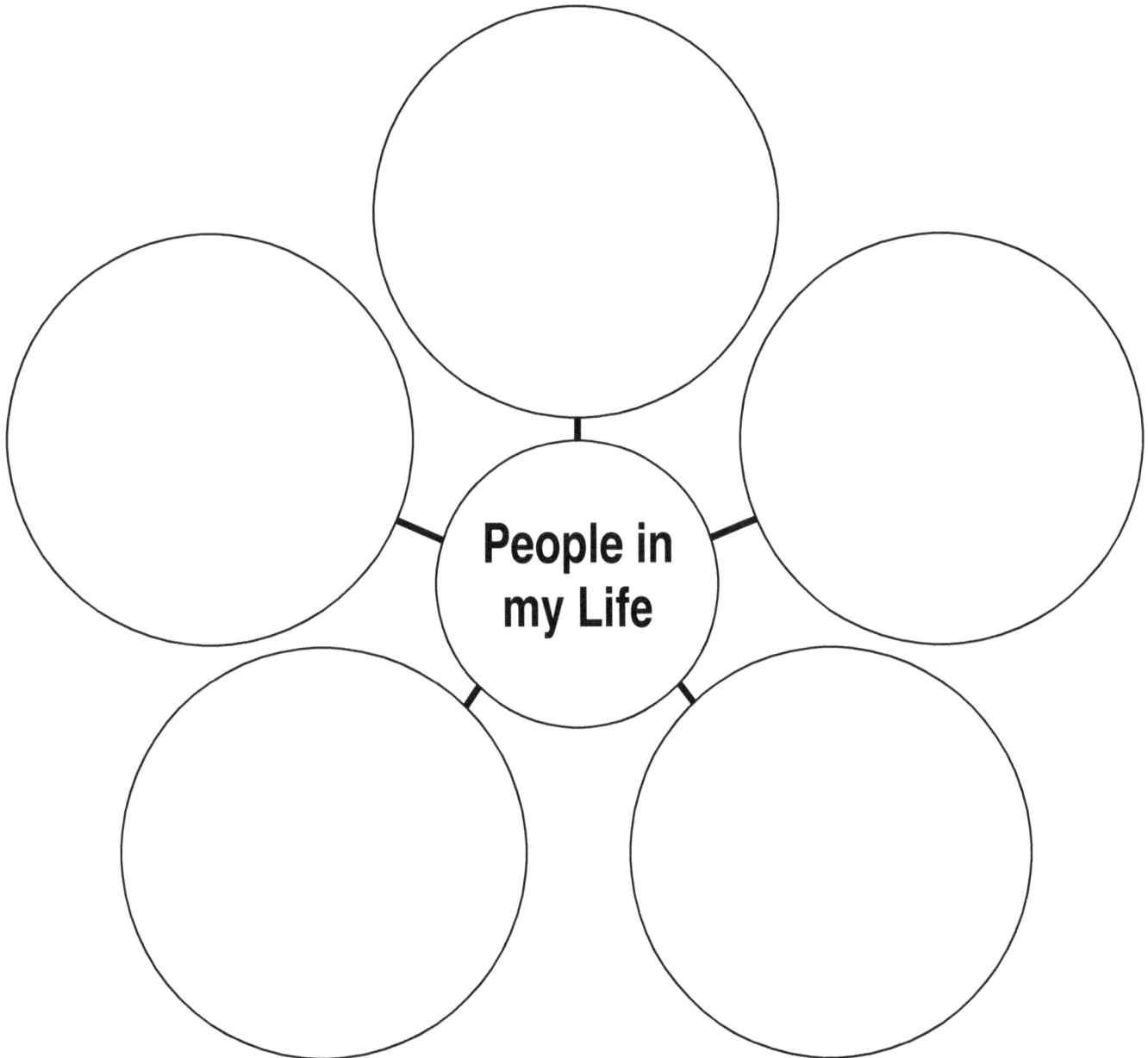

People in my Life

Admiration (Page 2)

Admiration is defined as respect or approval of another.

Now, in the circles below, list how people admire you as a human being in other things you do besides working. List the person and why you believe they admire you. USE NAME CODES.

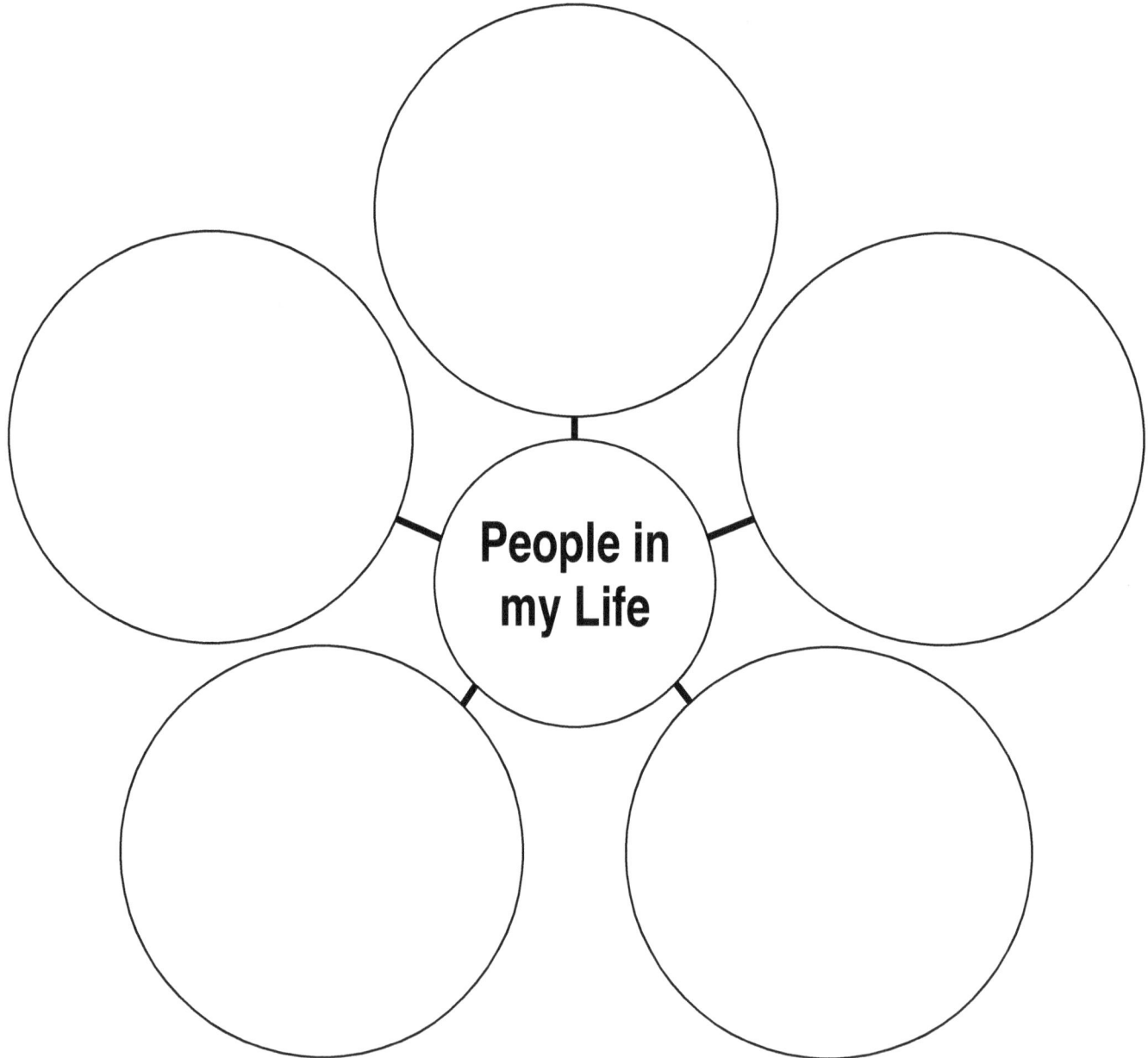

People in my Life

© 2023 WHOLE PERSON ASSOCIATES, 101 WEST 2ND STREET, SUITE 203, DULUTH MN 55802 • 800-247-6789 • WHOLEPERSON.COM

Work as a Coping Mechanism

Coping Mechanism: any strategy people use in the face of stress and trauma to help manage painful or difficult emotions.

Do you use work to cope with the uncertainties and stressors in your life? Complete the table below to identify the stressors and uncertainties in your life and how you use work as a coping mechanism.

Uncertainties and Stressors	Why Work Helps Me Cope	How I Worked to Cope
Example: Arguing with my partner about working too much.	*It gets me away from my partner to something I can control.*	*I told my partner I had to work late every night.*

For me, writing is a kind of coping mechanism.
~ Chuck Palahniuk

What type of work do you use as your coping mechanism?

_____

_____

_____

Control or Not?

Sense of Control: how much control you feel you have over your life.

Feeling a sense of control is critical to living with a sense of wellness. Having the right amount of control is what helps keep you balanced. Feeling that you have a lack of control can lead to overworking. Many people overwork to gain control over the uncontrollable aspects of their lives.

For each question below, explore your thoughts and feelings about how much control work provides you.

When was the last time you felt a lack of control outside work and turned to work for a sense of control?

_____

_____

What stress was occurring in your life?

_____

_____

Why did you turn to work for more control?

_____

_____

Did it help you? If so, how?

_____

_____

How else (other than working) could you have regained control?

_____

_____

Diligence leads to competence.
~ Jeffrey Benjamin

Authority Issues

Many people who have an addiction to work find themselves surrendering to authority figures in search of approval.

How do you surrender and compulsively work to try to please authority figures? Who are these primary authority figures, and how do you overwork to please them? Describe 3 of them below by placing the authority figure in the top square (USE NAME CODES) and how you overwork to get their approval in the squares below each authority figure.

Example:

IAJ

⇩

I volunteer for projects
I don't have time to do

I just remember that pivotal moment when you're a young adult,
and you realize that these authority figures are human beings, too,
and they're figuring out their lives just as you are, and they're flawed.
~ Gia Coppola

"I Am Competent" Sentence Starters

People who compulsively work often do so from the desire to fulfill basic psychological needs, such as a need to feel competent. Workaholics devote excessive time and mental energy working to feel competent, particularly if they don't feel so in other areas of their lives. How are you competent in the other areas of your life? *For example, you may be a great parent, an empathetic partner, a good softball player, etc.*

List the ways you are competent in the various aspects of your life.

I am competent as a _____. I can enhance this competence by:

_____

_____

_____

I am competent as a _____. I can enhance this competence by:

_____

_____

_____

I am competent as a _____. I can enhance this competence by:

_____

_____

_____

I am competent as a _____. I can enhance this competence by:

_____

_____

_____

© 2023 WHOLE PERSON ASSOCIATES, 101 WEST 2ND STREET, SUITE 203, DULUTH MN 55802 • 800-247-6789 • WHOLEPERSON.COM

Nobody is Perfect

Following are several definitions of perfectionism.

Perfectionism: the refusal to accept any standard short of perfection by making unreasonable, perfectionistic work demands of myself.

Perfectionism: perfectionism is a personality trait characterized by my striving for flawlessness and high-performance standards.

Perfectionism: the expectation that yourself and others achieve perfection.

In the following two tables, write about how you are too much of a perfectionist and how you expect others to be perfect. For example: you may expect yourself to achieve every goal you set. Similarly, you could expect your partner to make perfect decisions each time.

Perfectionism in Myself

I often expect myself to be perfect at work and in relationships. **Describe below.**

Ways I Try to Be Perfect	How I Show This Perfectionism	How I Can Learn to Accept My Imperfection

Perfectionism in Others

I often expect others to be perfect at work and in relationships. **Describe below.**

Ways I Want Others to Be Perfect	How I Want Them to Show This Perfectionism	How I Can Learn to Accept the Imperfection of Others

Escape Issues

Workaholics are often reliving patterns from their past. They use work to escape real-world issues, trauma, and feelings.

In the following spaces, identify some of the emotional issues or traumatic events you run from (death of a loved one, inability to communicate with your partner, divorce, serious illness, caring for aging parents, bullying, abuse, etc.). *Next to each one, identify the work pattern tied to the emotional issue or traumatic event* (working overtime to avoid facing the pain of being home).

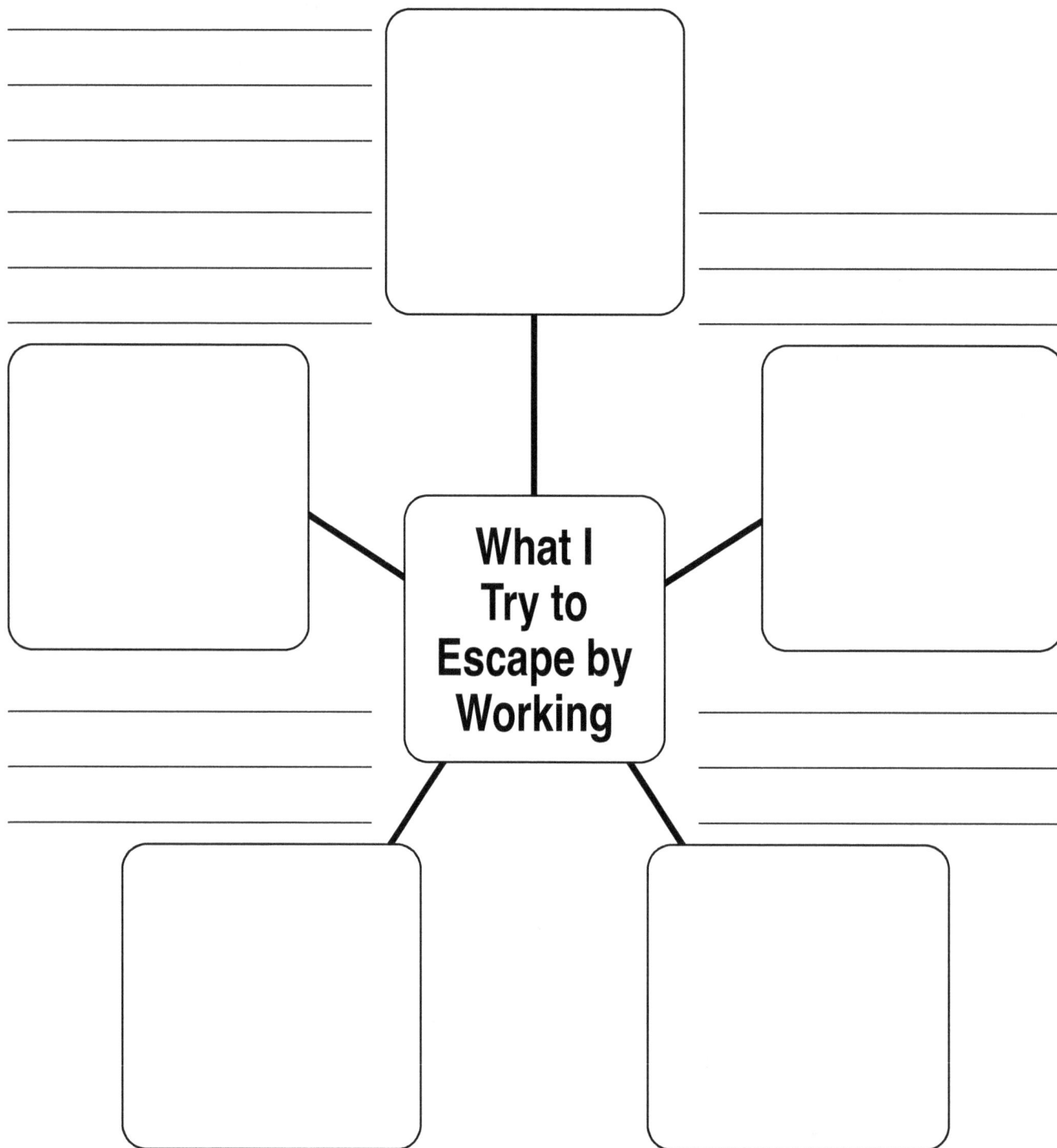

What I Try to Escape by Working

My Work Schedule

Work addicts tend to overwork most of the time. They feel good, in control, and accomplished when they're working. When they are not at work, they often obsess about it to the point that their lives are out of balance.

Days of the Week	Time I Spend Working or Thinking About Work	Time I Spend Doing Non-Work Activities
Example: Monday	I worked from 7 am to about 7 pm, then did additional work from 9 to 12.	I ate and played with my children from 7 to 9 pm and slept from midnight to 6 am.
Monday		
Tuesday		
Wednesday		
Thursday		
Friday		
Saturday		
Sunday		

Out of Balance

People addicted to work often find that their life is out of balance, negatively affecting their health, well-being, and relationships. How much time do you spend working each week?

Divide the circle below into sections (like a pie) that denote how many hours you are engaged during a typical week in work, family activities, hobbies, spiritual activities, community activities, educational activities, time with friends and pets, etc.

What changes can you make to start working less and engaging in non-work-related activities more often? Where can you begin spending more of your time?

_____

_____

In Balance

If you are addicted to work, you know that your life is out of balance, and you probably notice the effects on your health, well-being, and relationships.

Divide the circle below into sections (like a pie) that denote how many hours you would like to be engaged during a typical week in work, family activities, hobbies, spiritual activities, community activities, educational activities, and time with friends, pets, etc.

What specific steps will you take to begin working less and spending time with other people and other aspects of your life?

_____

_____

Lying About Work

If you overwork, you may have begun lying to others about your work behaviors. For example, to hide your work addiction, you may tell your friends or family members that you are shopping rather than coming home at dinner time or that you are surfing the web when you are secretly working.

What are some ways you lie to others so they do not know you are working?

People I Lie To	What I Tell Them	What I Am Really Doing

Things come apart so easily when they have been held together with lies.
~ Dorothy Allison

What is coming apart in your life because of your addiction to work?

_____

_____

Exaggerating and Minimizing

Many people who overwork lie to themselves about how much time they spend at work. To keep their image of a noble worker, they lie about their past failures, exaggerate their successes, and minimize or falsify their failures.

Think about ways you exaggerate your successes or minimize/falsify your failures. Write about them under the headings below. **BE HONEST!**

Exaggerated Successes	Minimized/Falsified Failures

If you tell the truth, you don't have to remember anything.
~ Mark Twain

Quotes about Workaholism

On the lines that follow each of the quotes, describe what the quote means to you and how it applies to your life.

I'm certainly not a workaholic.
~ Indira Gandhi

_____

_____

I'm a workaholic. Before long I'm traveling on my nervous energy alone.
This is incredibly exhausting.
~ Eva Gabor

_____

_____

Workaholics aren't heroes. They don't save the day, they just use it up. The real hero is home because she figured out a faster way.
~ Jason Fried

_____

_____

If you enjoy being at work more than being at home it doesn't mean you are a workaholic, it simply means you are in love with your work and you worship it.
~ honeya

_____

_____

Which quote speaks to you the most? Write why it touches you?

_____

_____

_____

_____

_____

_____

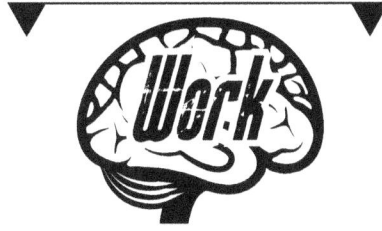

Work Patterns

Name _____

Date _____

Work Patterns Assessment
Introduction and Directions

Many people addicted to work and work-related behavior do not fully recognize the patterns that lead to a problem. They usually live in denial and choose not to see how their work affects them and the people in their lives. Awareness of these patterns can be the starting point of recovery.

The following assessment contains 20 statements related to excessive work behavior. This assessment can help you gauge the extent to which working is a problem in your life.

Read each of the statements and decide whether it describes you. If the statement describes you, circle the number in the YES column next to that item. If the statement does not describe you, circle the number in the NO column next to that item.

In the following example, the circled 2 indicates that the person completing this assessment believes that the statement is true for them:

	YES	NO
When it comes to working, I notice that …		
I am busier without increasing my productivity	(2)	1
I think obsessively about freeing up more time for work	(2)	1

This is not a test. Since there are no right or wrong answers, do not spend too much time thinking about your answers. Be sure to respond to every statement. The purpose of this assessment is for YOU to learn more about YOU and your work habits.

BE HONEST!

If you choose, no one else needs to see the results.

(Turn to the next page and begin.)

Work Patterns Assessment

Name _____ Date _____

This will only be accurate if you respond honestly. No one else needs to see this if you choose.

	YES	NO

When it comes to working, I notice that ...

	YES	NO
I am busier without increasing my productivity	2	1
I think obsessively about freeing up more time for work.	2	1
I am spending more time working than I intended	2	1
I have an excessive need to use work to define my self-worth.	2	1
I am working a lot to reduce feelings of sadness	2	1
I ignore suggestions that I should cut down on work	2	1
Our family has problems resulting from my overworking.	2	1
I am experiencing health problems that may be caused by work stress	2	1
I need to work more than before to get the same buzz	2	1
I become stressed and cranky if I am prevented from working.	2	1
My family tells me I spend more time working than with them	2	1
Problems are developing in my social life	2	1
I am unable to set work limits or quit work for the day	2	1
I have a difficult time enjoying the fruits of my labors	2	1
I am unable to be happy despite financial success	2	1
I break promises to get together with friends so I can work	2	1
I find it difficult to delegate work. I want to do it all, so it's done right	2	1
When I go to a social activity, I don't enjoy it and want to go to work.	2	1
I am unable to relax and disengage from work	2	1
My mental health is deteriorating due to the pressures of overwork	2	1

Work Patterns TOTAL = _____

The more answers from the YES column you circled, the greater your risk of experiencing a problem with your work-related behavior.

Go to the next page for scoring assessment results, profile interpretation, and individual description.

Work Patterns Assessment

Scoring Directions and Profile Interpretations

The assessment you just completed is designed to measure the impact your work behavior is having on your life.

For each of the items in the three sections on the previous page, count the scores you circled. Put each of those totals on the TOTAL spot at the end of each section. Then, transfer your totals to the space below:

Work Patterns TOTAL   =   _____

Assessment Profile Interpretation

By circling even ONE answer from the YES column, you might risk developing or having a full-blown work addiction. The more answers from the YES column you circled, the greater your risk of experiencing a problem with your work-related behavior.

Work Patterns TOTAL   =   _____

This assessment measures the impact of overworking on your life. The HIGHER your score on the Work Patterns Assessment, the more you need to take care of yourself, and live a balanced home, social, family, and work life.

Enter your score on the line below.

20 = Low	**30 = Moderate**	**40 = High**

What is your reaction to your score?

_____

_____

_____

Type A Personality?

Many workaholics have a Type A personality. People with a Type A personality are motivated by work and achievements.

For each Type A personality trait listed below that you can relate to, journal about how you have demonstrated that trait.

I can be aggressive at times.

_____

_____

I am ambitious.

_____

_____

I can be controlling.

_____

_____

I am competitive.

_____

_____

I lack patience.

_____

_____

I am preoccupied with status.

_____

_____

I can be hostile at times.

_____

_____

I become terribly stressed when I don't achieve success.

_____

_____

I would rather work than do pretty much anything else.

_____

_____

Obsessed with Work?

Obsession: a persistent disturbing preoccupation with an
unreasonable idea or feeling compelling motivation.

In the boxes below, identify reasons you become obsessed with your work. In the center of the graphic, write how they affect your life.

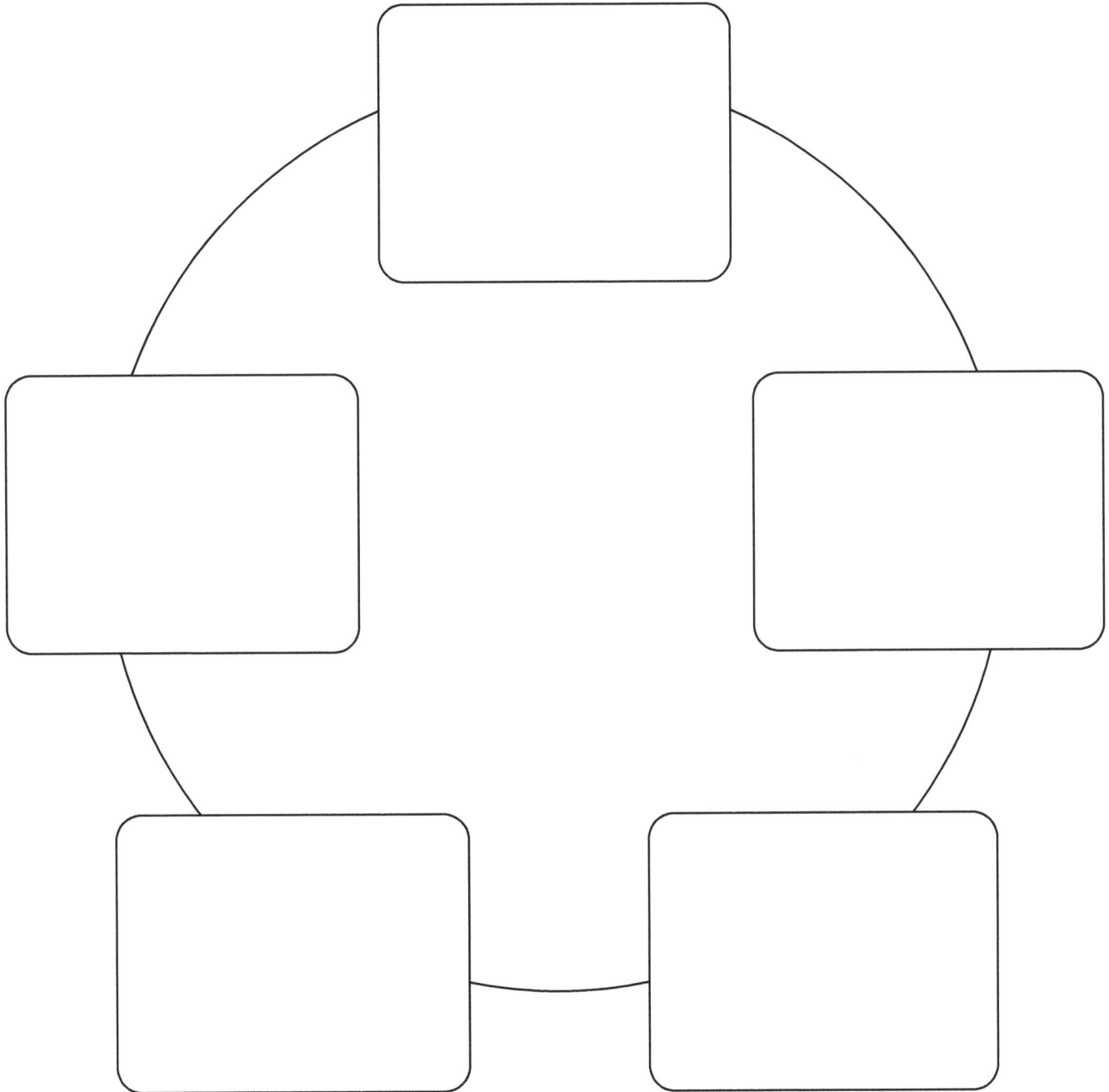

An obsession is where something will not leave your mind.
~ Eric Clapton

What Have You Given Up?

Have you reduced your participation in other recreational activities due to work?

Below, write about what specific activities you have given up due to your work addiction.

I have given up _____ (family activity) because ...

_____

_____

I have given up _____ (recreational activity) because ...

_____

_____

I have given up _____ (spiritual/religious activity) because ...

_____

_____

I have given up _____ (friendship activity) because ...

_____

_____

I have given up _____ (fun activity) because ...

_____

_____

Something else I have given up is _____ because ...

_____

_____

Something else I have given up is _____ because ...

_____

_____

 © 2023 WHOLE PERSON ASSOCIATES, 101 WEST 2ND STREET, SUITE 203, DULUTH MN 55802 • 800-247-6789 • WHOLEPERSON.COM

Meeting My Needs

People addicted to work often feel that working is the only way to meet their needs.

Respond to each statement by journaling about your own experiences.

Working meets my social needs by:

_____

_____

    Other ways I could meet my social needs: _____

    _____

    _____

Working meets my self-esteem needs by:

_____

_____

    Other ways I could meet my self-esteem needs: _____

    _____

    _____

Working meets my life purpose needs by:

_____

_____

    Other ways I could meet my life purpose needs:_____

    _____

    _____

How Do You Overwork?

People with a work addiction overwork in many different ways. How do you overwork?

List your title, profession, trade, etc. on the line above the table. On the right side of the table, describe how you overwork in various environments.

My work_____

How I Overwork at the Office	
How I Overwork at Home	
How I Overwork Using Technology	
Other Ways I Overwork	

I Would Rather Work Than ...

This page will help you explore why you would rather work than engage in other life activities.

Complete each sentence fragment by writing about your experiences with work.

I would rather work than _____ because ...

_____

_____

_____

_____

I would rather work than _____ because ...

_____

_____

_____

_____

I would rather work than _____ because ...

_____

_____

_____

_____

I would rather work than _____ because ...

_____

_____

_____

_____

The Basket of Work

For workaholics, all the eggs of self-esteem are in the basket of work.
~ Judith M Bardwick

Let's look at the eggs in your basket of work to build your self-esteem. List what you are proud of in the non-work areas of your life in the middle column. List ways to appreciate yourself and build more self-esteem in the right column.

Non-Work Areas of My Life	I Am Proud of ...	Ways to Appreciate Myself and Build More Self-Esteem in This Area
Example: Family	*My skills in the kitchen*	*Host a dinner party for my friends*
Family		
Friends		
Community / Volunteering		
Education / Training		
Spirituality / Religion		
Other		

© 2023 WHOLE PERSON ASSOCIATES, 101 WEST 2ND STREET, SUITE 203, DULUTH MN 55802 • 800-247-6789 • WHOLEPERSON.COM

What Triggers Your Need to Work?

People addicted to work will find it enlightening to identify what triggers their need to work.

Below, explore your circumstances, the people around you, and the thoughts that go through your mind when you feel the need to work. Then write thoughts that could change your thinking.

Example:

The Circumstance	The People Around Me	The Thoughts in My Head
Example: I'm bored. There is nothing to do.	My family is all doing their own thing and ignoring me.	I may as well go to work early. I feel that I am not needed at home.

Thoughts I could have to change my way of thinking about work:

Example: "What others are doing has nothing to do with how much I work." "I could clean the closet that I've neglected." "I can call a friend." "I can go to the gym and work out." "I can go to the movie I want to see."

Now, create two of your own scenarios:

The Circumstance	The People Around Me	The Thoughts in My Head

Thoughts I could have to change my way of thinking about work:

_____

_____

The Circumstance	The People Around Me	The Thoughts in My Head

Thoughts I could have to change my way of thinking about work:

_____

_____

Break Promises?

Because workaholics obsess about their work, they often break promises to themselves, their family, friends, co-workers, etc. Their broken promises often relate to the amount of time they work, their travel schedules, and other employment-related activities.

Below, identify some of the promises you have broken and to whom. BE HONEST!

A Promise I Made	To Whom **USE NAME CODES**	Why I Broke the Promise
Example: I promised my family that we would spend a week at Disneyland after school let out. I broke the promise, and they were heartbroken and angry.	*MDJ, MSS, MWD, MDF, GMF, GPD*	*My boss asked me to do a project. He said everyone else who could do it already had plans. I thought he would give me a bonus or a raise and would think highly of me. He didn't.*

Promises mean everything, but after they are broken, they mean nothing.
~ Unknown

I Should Work

Workaholics often differ from people who are highly engaged in their jobs and love their work. Some workaholics do not especially enjoy their work; they feel compelled to work because of pressures they put on themselves or pressures people put on them. They work because they feel like they should or ought to or because they will gain favor from the boss or others.

Example:
I should work as much as possible because *I want a way to gain my partner's approval. I feel guilty because my partner makes more money than I do and constantly reminds me of it.*

> **Is this a good reason?** *No* **Why or why not?** *Even if I don't work overtime, I am still bringing in a decent income.*

I should work as much as possible because _____

_____

_____

Is this a good reason?_____ Why or why not? _____

_____

I should work as much as possible because _____

_____

_____

Is this a good reason?_____ Why or why not? _____

_____

I should work as much as possible because _____

_____

_____

Is this a good reason?_____ Why or why not? _____

_____

I should work as much as possible because _____

_____

_____

Is this a good reason?_____ Why or why not? _____

_____

Not Getting It Done?

Workaholics tend to neglect people as well as other aspects of their lives. They are so busy working that they have no time to care for their emotional, mental, and physical well-being.

What aspects of life do you ignore because of your need to work? Write, draw, or doodle your thoughts in the spaces below:

Relationships	Home
Emotional, Mental, and Physical Well-Being	*Fun*

Are You Honest with Yourself?

Workaholics are usually not honest about how much time they spend at work and why. They do not consider if it is essential to work longer than usual, work extra hours to accomplish objectives, or stay late for other reasons. Some reasons they do this are to impress their boss or co-workers, achieve perfection, want to do it all, or want to be alone. They believe they are their jobs and are unable or unwilling to reduce their workload.

In the hexagons below, identify some of the times you have overworked. Dig deeply! Next to each hexagon identify the TRUE reasons you overworked.

Why I Overwork

It's Emotional

People addicted to work would rather be working than doing almost anything else. Some even experience challenging emotions like anxiety, apprehension, guilt, or shame when they are not working.

What challenging emotions do you experience when you're not working? Describe them and why you believe you feel them.

Emotions I Experience		Why I Believe that I Feel This Way
Example: I feel uneasy.	⇨	*I keep thinking of what I would rather be doing at work instead.*
	⇨	
	⇨	
	⇨	
	⇨	
	⇨	
	⇨	
	⇨	
	⇨	

All emotions are pure which gather you and lift you up; that emotion is impure which seizes only one side of your being and so distorts you.
~ Rainer Maria Rilke

Expectations

Workaholics tend to work beyond what is reasonably expected of them. They may work overtime a lot, not take vacations, go to work when sick, say yes to extra work for no pay, take work home at night, work on the weekends, work with technology on non-work hours, etc.

Do you go beyond the expectations others have of you?

Identify the times you have worked beyond reasonable expectations at your place of employment. If you can't think of the times you exceeded those expectations, ask the people you live with.

A Work Expectation	A Way I Went Above And Beyond Expectations	What I Gave Up
Example: I am contracted to work 8 am to 5 pm five days a week.	I worked on a project over the entire weekend and even brought my meals to the office.	Time with my children to go to the zoo and enjoy an activity at our place of worship.

I'm at the point in my life where I don't want to work as hard.
Actually, I've had to take a good hard look at workaholism
and its effect on one's mental health.
~ Alan Ball

I'm a Workaholic ...

Take a look at the following workaholism quote, and respond to the questions.

I'm a workaholic, so I ignore the signs of fatigue and just keep going and going,
and then conk out when I get home. It can be pretty stressful.
~ Keke Palmer

How does this quote relate to your work life?

_____
_____
_____

What signs of fatigue are you experiencing? How are you dealing with them?

_____
_____
_____

Why do you tend to keep going and going?

_____
_____
_____

Are you planning to keep on going and going?

_____
_____
_____

How can you begin to take time to relax so you don't conk out when you get home?

_____
_____
_____

How can you develop and maintain more life balance?

_____
_____
_____

Quotes about Overwork

Read all three of the quotations below.

#1

When I look back on what I've done, I think I'm drawn to obsession, perhaps.
~ Christopher Guest

#2

Promises are like crying babies in a theater, they should be carried out at once.
~ Norman Vincent Peale

#3

The sign of an intelligent people is their ability to control their emotions
by the application of reason.
~ Marya Mannes

Pick a quote that sounds like you and explain why. #_____

_____

_____

_____

Pick one that inspires you to do better and explain how you will do that. #_____

_____

_____

_____

Pick a quote that taught you something and explain what it taught you. #_____

_____

_____

_____

Write your very own quote regarding work and what you have learned.

_____

_____

_____

I Have a Problem

Name _____

Date _____

The Work Addiction Workbook — **I HAVE A PROBLEM**

I Have a Problem Assessment
Introduction and Directions

Behavioral addictions constitute any maladaptive pattern of excessive behavior that manifests in physiological, psychological, and cognitive symptoms.

When people have an addiction to work, they experience the same symptoms as someone addicted to substances.

The *I Have a Problem Assessment* contains fourteen statements of symptoms that may be related to someone who is addicted to work. These symptoms are indicators of someone who has a problem.

Read each statement and decide whether or not it describes you. If the statement is TRUE, circle the number next to that item in the TRUE column. If it is FALSE, circle the number next to that item in the FALSE column.

In the following example, the circled number 2 in the TRUE column indicates the statement is true of the person completing the inventory:

When it comes to working ...
Continuance

	TRUE	FALSE
I am continuing to overwork even though it is creating or exacerbating physical and psychological problems	(2)	1
I am continuing to overwork even though it is creating interpersonal problems	(2)	1

This is not a test. Since there are no right or wrong answers, do not spend too much time thinking about your answers. Be sure to respond to every statement. The purpose of this assessment is for YOU to learn more about YOU and your work habits.

BE HONEST!

If you choose, no one else needs to see the results.

(Turn to the next page and begin.)

I Have a Problem Assessment

Name _____ Date _____

This will only be accurate if you respond honestly. No one else needs to see this if you choose.

When it comes to working ...   TRUE   FALSE

Continuance

I am continuing to overwork even though it is creating or
exacerbating physical and psychological problems 2 1

I am continuing to overwork even though it is creating
interpersonal problems...2 1

Intention effects

I regularly neglect my commitments so I can work more 2 1

I consistently work beyond what I intend 2 1

Lack of control

I have unsuccessfully attempted to reduce my work hours.................2 1

I tried to ease up by working overtime on the weekends,
but I was unsuccessful 2 1

Reduction in activities

As a direct result of my work behavior, my social and familial
activities occur less often or have stopped.............................2 1

As a direct result of my work behavior, my recreational activities
with friends occur less often or have stopped 2 1

Time

I spend a great deal of time preparing for, engaging in, and
recovering from working...2 1

I spend a great deal of time preoccupied with my work 2 1

Tolerance

I constantly feel the need to increase the amount of work I do
to feel productive 2 1

I no longer have a sense of accomplishment or satisfaction
from working just eight hours a day.....................................2 1

Withdrawal

In the absence of work, I experience negative effects such as
anxiety and irritability when I am with other people 2 1

In the absence of work, I experience negative issues
such as restlessness and sleep problems 2 1

I HAVE A PROBLEM TOTAL = _____

Go to the next page for scoring assessment results, profile interpretation, and individual description.

I Have a Problem Assessment

Scoring Directions and Profile Interpretations

The assessment you just completed is designed to help you explore your level of work addiction and your work-related behaviors.

Total the scores you circled on the I Have a Problem Assessment and transfer that number below:

I Have a Problem TOTAL = _____

Assessment Profile Interpretation

Place your score on the line below and then profile it by placing an X on the continuum line below. The higher your score, the more intense your problem is.

14 = Low	21 = Moderate	28 = High

Inside of every problem lies an opportunity.
~ Robert Kiyosaki

What ideas do you have to turn your problem into an opportunity?

_____

_____

_____

_____

_____

*Share your ideas with your professional or with
other participants in your group.*

Organizing My Life Around Work

Workaholics are constantly trying to free up more time to work, which means they are taking time away from being with family and friends. They may not be interested in a vacation unless it is a working vacation. They may try to organize their lives to allow them to work more rather than less. By not taking a break, their work is often not up to par because of burnout.

In the hexagons below, identify the ways you organize your life to work even more.

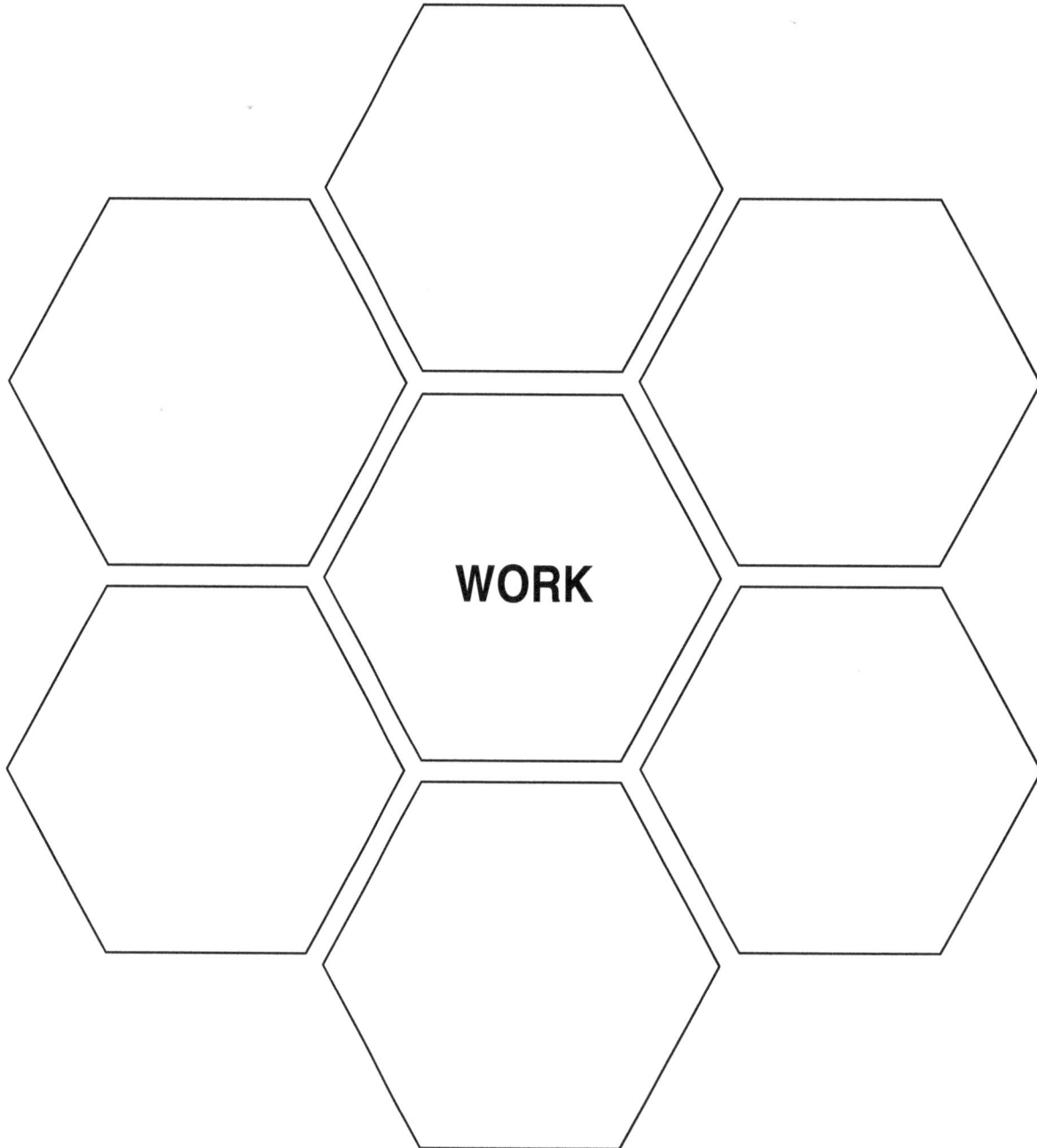

WORK

Are your responses fair to your family, friends, workplace, or yourself?

_____

_____

Role Interpretation

One of the biggest challenges for people addicted to anything is developing and maintaining a good feeling about themselves in other areas of their lives. Workaholics are usually good at their work, enjoy it, and feel that it meets their needs. They focus solely on work and neglect other areas and people.

Many workaholics minimize or ignore the other roles in their life. Identify your non-work roles (whether you want to be involved or not).

Explore how you think others see you and how you can do better in that role.

My Roles	How Others See Me (USE NAME CODES)	How I Can Do Better
Example: *Relative*	*MSJ thinks I'm a pretty good brother, but he'd like to spend more time with me.*	*I could show more interest in my brother's life by calling him once a week.*
Relative		
Partner		
Co-worker		
Homemaker		
Provider		
Caregiver		
Home Repairer		
Other		
Other		

Can You Say No?

At home, it can be easy to say no. However, whether it's a co-worker or supervisor asking you to lead an extra project, organize a retreat, or leave for a conference the next morning, remember that it's okay to say no at work. Stop accepting tasks out of guilt or a false sense of obligation. You will have more time for meaningful activities such as spending time with family, watching movies with friends, or going out to dinner with a significant other.

Below, identify situations at work when you could not say no, why you were unable to do so, and how you could have been more assertive. Remember – being assertive is being open, honest, and direct. Not rude or aggressive. Assertiveness conveys that you are an individual and have a life outside of work.

When I Could Not Say No (USE NAME CODES)	Why I Could Not Say No	How I Could Have Been More Assertive
Example: MBJ called me at home and asked me to pick up a package at 11 pm at a warehouse.	I felt obligated even though I had worked from 6 am to 7 pm that day.	I could have told MBJ I had obligations at home and suggested he call UBER to make the pick-up.

Ways NOT to Say No:
- Passive Approach: Saying no might sound like "Ok, I'll do it...this time" or "I guess I can."
- Aggressive Approach: Saying no might be "I told you no!" or "What makes you think I'd do that?"
- Passive-Aggressive Approach: Saying no might sound like "Fine" or "I'll get back to you."

Ways to Assertively Say No at Work:
- "I am grateful for the opportunity and for you thinking of me. However, I am booked with a commitment I made months ago."
- "I can't this time. I have kids waiting for me at home to play ball. Thank you for thinking of me."
- "I am so flattered that you asked, but unfortunately, I cannot do that. Can I help you think of someone who might be able to help?"

Escaping My Challenging Emotions (Page 1)

Workaholics often overwork to reduce feelings such as inadequacy, loneliness, guilt, anxiety, helplessness, hopelessness, fear, anger, or sadness. In essence, work provides a means of escape for workaholics. If they're doing their job, they can avoid uncomfortable emotions.

Place a checkmark in front of the emotions you try to escape. Describe why you feel this way. Think of some other ways you can deal with these emotions.

☐ **Inadequacy – Why I feel this way:** _____

_____

How else can I deal with this emotion? _____

_____

☐ **Loneliness – Why I feel this way:** _____

_____

How else can I deal with this emotion? _____

_____

☐ **Guilt – Why I feel this way:** _____

_____

How else can I deal with this emotion? _____

_____

☐ **Shame – Why I feel this way:** _____

_____

How else can I deal with this emotion? _____

_____

☐ **Helplessness or Hopelessness – Why I feel this way:** _____

_____

How else can I deal with this emotion? _____

_____

Escaping My Challenging Emotions (Page 2)

☐ **Sadness – Why I feel this way:** _____

_____

    How else can I deal with this emotion? _____

_____

☐ **Boredom – Why I feel this way:** _____

_____

    How else can I deal with this emotion? _____

_____

☐ **Fear – Why I feel this way:** _____

_____

    How else can I deal with this emotion? _____

_____

☐ **Anger – Why I feel this way:** _____

_____

    How else can I deal with this emotion? _____

_____

☐ **Other – Why I feel this way:** _____

_____

    How else can I deal with this emotion? _____

_____

Who is a trusted professional, family member, or friend who can help you learn to deal with

challenging emotions? _____

_____

Apply Limits

People addicted to working tend to work more than the average amount of time expected. If this is the case for you, you must limit your hours.

TO APPLY LIMITS:
- Set aside one or more days of the week, such as Saturday or Sunday, as rest days.
- Be strict in not working at work or home on your rest days.
- Unplug from all technology.
- Set specific hours when you do not allow yourself to work.
- Do not take on extra work or bring work home on the day before a rest day.
- Set manageable goals for each rest day: nap, play ball with the kids, help your significant other make dinner, read a book, take a walk to the park with family, watch a game, etc.

Inside the squares, write the ways you will begin to set limits on the time you spend with work. Beside each limit, write about how you will ensure that you will stick to it.

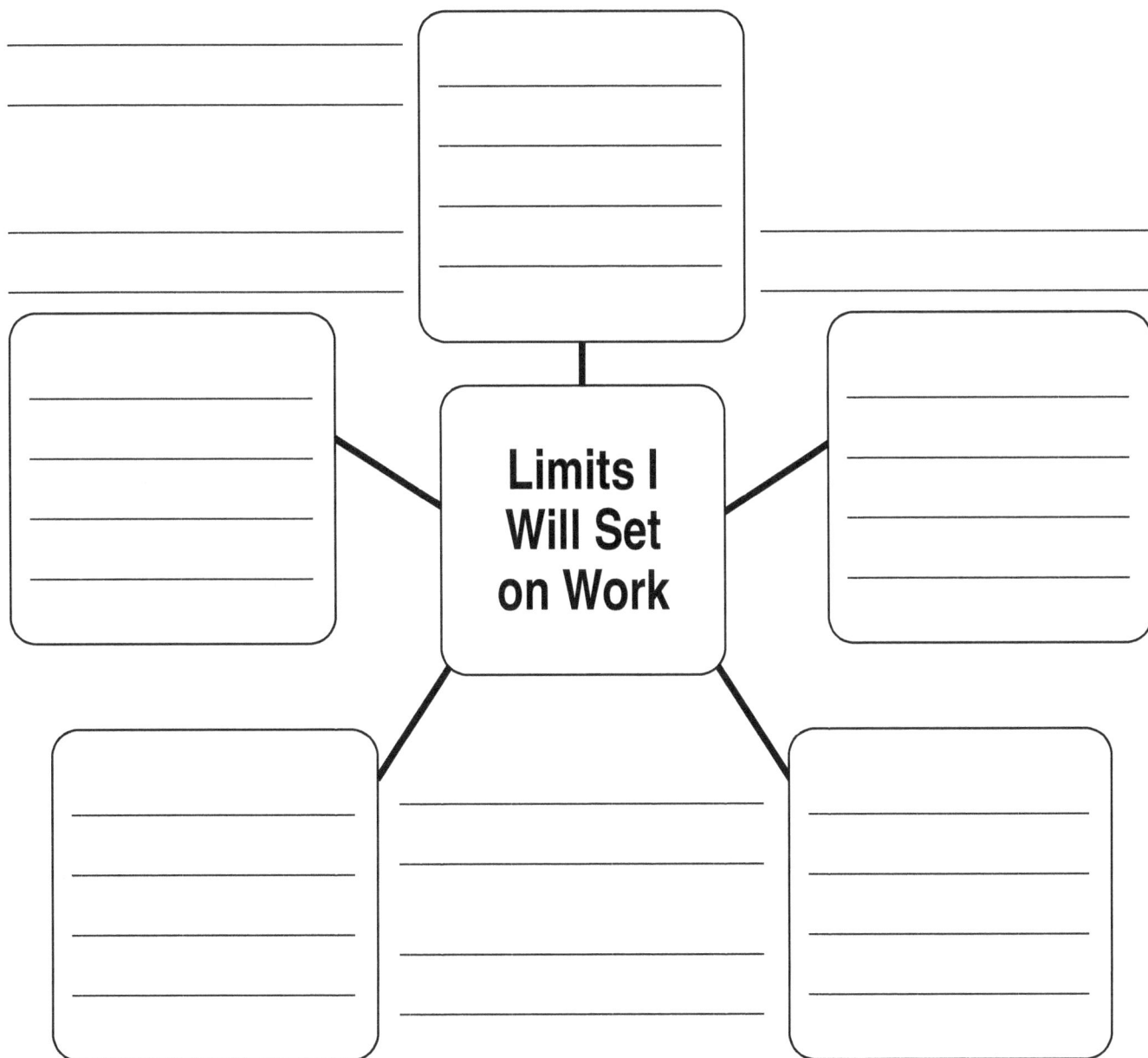

Limits I Will Set on Work

I Will Not Listen

Workaholics usually do not listen when people tell them to cut down on their work.

Below, describe situations in which someone told you to work less. In the cloud, write what the person said and their concern. In the burst, write your rationale for continuing to work.

Situation:

_____

_____

_____

_____

Situation:

_____

_____

_____

_____

 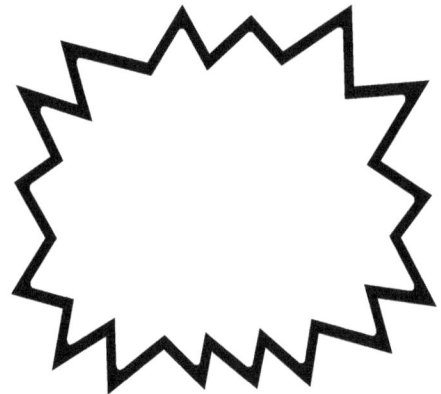

Situation:

_____

_____

_____

_____

Liar, Liar!

Workaholics are like other addicts. Like other addicts who try to hide their addiction, a workaholic might lie. For example, they might sneak out of bed in the middle of the night to work on a project without anyone knowing it or lie about how many hours they spent in the office. Workaholics may work and then lie about it to get out of things they don't want to do. Lying about work hours can be a significant problem and a major source of stress in relationships.

What are some of the ways you have lied or deceived others in order to work?

Times I Lied or Deceived	Why I Lied or Deceived	Who My Lie Hurt
Example: I told my partner that I HAD to work on Saturdays.	I did not want to go to my son's football games.	I worked even though I did not NEED to. My son was disappointed in me. Our relationship was weakened.

Lying is like alcoholism. You are always recovering.
~ Steven Soderbergh

What does the Soderberg quote mean to you?

_____

_____

_____

_____

I'm Stressed

Workaholics usually become stressed if they are prohibited from working. They are not likely to relax on a beach, read a mystery novel, or unwind with a round of golf. In fact, being away from work is likely to cause more anxiety.

Which activities stress you out and make you anxious because they prevent you from working? Below, write about those activities and why they affect you so powerfully.

Family	
Friends	
Sports	
Religious/Spiritual	
Community	
Recreational	
Social	
Educational	
Fitness	
Other	
Other	

© 2023 WHOLE PERSON ASSOCIATES, 101 WEST 2ND STREET, SUITE 203, DULUTH MN 55802 • 800-247-6789 • WHOLEPERSON.COM

Non-Work Activities

Workaholics tend to deprioritize hobbies, leisure activities, or exercise because of their need to work. Although workaholics might say it's important to relax, exercise, engage in hobbies, or spend time with family and friends, they still cannot make or find time for these activities. Work remains the top priority at all times.

In each block below, write about, draw, or doodle a hobby, leisure activity, relaxing activity, and an exercise regimen you would be willing to incorporate into your week.

Hobby	**Leisure Activity**
Relaxing Activity	**Exercise Regimen**

Health Problems

Workaholics experience many health-related problems because of their work. They often experience mental and physical health problems stemming from pushing themselves to work for long hours. Some problems are listed below.

For each one, write about how you have been affected from working too much.

Health Problem	How It Is Affecting Me	Why I Am Experiencing the Problem
Example: Lack of sleep	*I am only sleeping 3 to 5 hours per night.*	*I can't keep work ideas from popping into my head. I get up to write them down and then can't fall asleep.*
Lack of Sleep		
High Levels of Stress		
Strained Relationships		
Anxiety		
Sadness		
High Blood Pressure		
Migraines		
Heart Problems		
Fatigue		
Other		

Projects

Workaholics want to do everything themselves. They often take sole responsibility for a work project rather than delegating to other people.

Write about a current or past work project in the space provided. Name the project, then in the circles below, describe to whom and how you could delegate some tasks and responsibilities.

A Current Project _____

Ways I Could Delegate Some Aspects of the Project to Others:

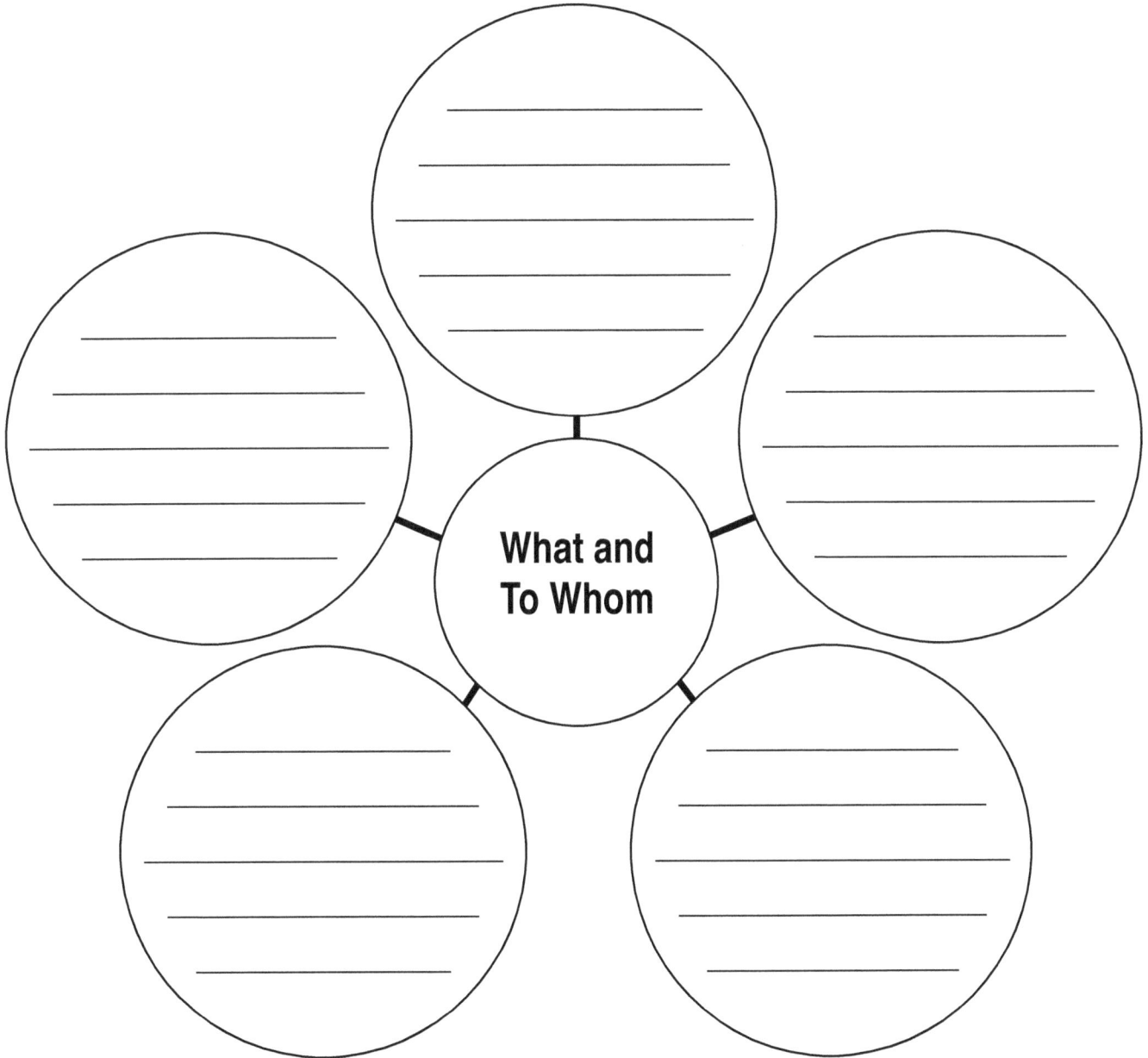

What and To Whom

What stops you from doing this?

_____

_____

I Believe

Many people addicted to work have certain beliefs that motivate and drive them to want to work even more. Even though some of these beliefs may be inaccurate, they may contribute to the desire to work more.

With each of the sentence starters below, write your beliefs about work.

I believe that my working will _____

_____

I believe that if I keep working I will _____

_____

I believe that if I stop working I will _____

_____

I believe that through work, I can solve the problem of _____

_____

I believe that by working, my family _____

_____

I believe that the more money I make _____

_____

I believe that only by working can I _____

_____

Who is a trusted individual (therapist, relative, clergy, friend, medical doctor, parent, etc.) with whom you can go over your responses from this page and talk about them, in confidence? (USE NAME CODES)

_____

_____

Ways I'm Competitive

Many workaholics have the type of personality that drives them to be competitive and want to be the best at everything. No one likes to lose, but for a competitive person, it can be especially disappointing to see someone else win. Work addicts who are competitive like to compete in all aspects of their lives, not only at work. In their personal lives, they may compete to find out who is most intelligent, reads the most, runs fastest, can eat the most hotdogs, can swim the fastest, be the best golfer, etc.

On the lines that follow, list some of the ways you are competitive at work, and some of the ways you are competitive in other areas of your life.

At Work	In My Personal Life
_____	_____
_____	_____
_____	_____
_____	_____
_____	_____
_____	_____
_____	_____
_____	_____
_____	_____
_____	_____
_____	_____
_____	_____

Being competitive can be great when it helps you push yourself. It helps to build strong alliances and good relationships, and to know when to cooperate. When taken too far, it can become a problem and put you at odds with co-workers. Often, feelings of competitiveness are triggered by jealousy.

Stop comparing yourself to others. Be yourself.
Say to yourself, "It's okay not to always win!"

A To-Do List

Workaholics get excited about work and working. They usually become more excited about work than about family or other activities. They can't seem to get enough work. When one project or task is complete, there is always another waiting on their to-do list. The problem is that they usually do not make a to-do list for their spare time and family activities.

Below, make a to-do list for all your non-work interests. Items on your list can be for family (take son fishing), *friends* (go out to dinner), *recreation* (learn to play a musical instrument), *etc.*

My To-Do List

Awareness of Problem Behavior

People addicted to work are often unaware of how much time they actually work.

On the line under each symptom, place an X on the continuum of how much you relate to the statement. On the dotted line below each one, write why you rated yourself that way. BE HONEST!

I work much more than 40 hours a week.

_____
0 (Not Aware)   5 (Somewhat Aware)   10 (Very Aware)

I am impatient with those who have priorities other than work.

_____
0 (Not Aware)   5 (Somewhat Aware)   10 (Very Aware)

I work long hours at the expense of family or other relationships.

_____
0 (Not Aware)   5 (Somewhat Aware)   10 (Very Aware)

I think about work when going to sleep, driving, or when others are talking.

_____
0 (Not Aware)   5 (Somewhat Aware)   10 (Very Aware)

I become irritated when others take my attention from my work.

_____
0 (Not Aware)   5 (Somewhat Aware)   10 (Very Aware)

I prefer spending my time at work over most everything else in my life.

_____
0 (Not Aware)   5 (Somewhat Aware)   10 (Very Aware)

Awareness is the key to knowing that you have a problem with overworking.

_____
0 (Not Aware)   5 (Somewhat Aware)   10 (Very Aware)

HIGHER (Very Aware) scores on each of the statements indicates that you have an acute awareness of your problem.

MIDDLE (Somewhat Aware) scores indicate that you are somewhat aware that you have a problem in these areas.

LOWER (Not Aware) scores indicate that you are not very conscious of a problem in these areas and suggest that you might need to be open to your work addiction.

Quotes about Problem Working Behaviors

On the lines that follow each of the quotes, describe what the quote means to you and how it applies to your work addiction issues.

Assertiveness is not what you do, it's who you are!
~ Shakti Gawain

_____

_____

I'm very, very competitive. If my grandmother asks to race me down the street, I'm going to try to beat her. And I'll probably enjoy it!
~ Derek Jeter

_____

_____

There is a fine line between assertiveness and being relaxed.
~ Justin Guarini

_____

_____

There are so many emotions that you're feeling, you can get stifled by them if you're feeling them all at once. What I try to do is take one moment - one simple, simple feeling - and expand it into three-and-a-half minutes.
~ Taylor Swift

_____

_____

Write your own quotation about what you think about your work issues.

_____

_____

_____

_____

_____

_____

Work

Maintain Wellness

Name _____

Date _____

Job Assessment
Introduction and Directions

Job Burnout: A state of emotional, physical, and mental exhaustion caused by excessive and prolonged work stress that also involves a sense of reduced accomplishment and loss of personal identity. It occurs when one is feeling overwhelmed, emotionally drained, and unable to meet constant demands.

People addicted to work, work, and more work, are at risk of burning out unless they can maintain a sense of wellness.

The *Job Assessment* contains 20 statements related to people who overwork because they enjoy the work or feel compelled to work. This assessment can help you explore how close you are to burning out from working too much and too long. Awareness is key to controlling a work addiction.

Read each statement and decide whether it does or does not describe you. If the statement describes you, circle the number in the TRUE column next to that item. If the statement does not describe you, circle the number in the NOT TRUE column next to that item.

In the following example, the circled 2 indicates that the person completing this assessment believes that the statement is true:

	TRUE	**NOT TRUE**
I notice that more often:		
I have a negative attitude at work	(2)	1
I dread going to work	(2)	1

This is not a test. Since there are no right or wrong answers, do not spend too much time thinking about your answers. Be sure to respond to every statement. The purpose of this assessment is for YOU to learn more about YOU and your work habits.

BE HONEST!

If you choose, no one else needs to see the results.

(Turn to the next page and begin.)

Job Assessment

Name _____ Date _____

This will only be accurate if you respond honestly. No one else needs to see this if you choose.

I notice that more often:	TRUE	NOT TRUE
I have a negative attitude at work	2	1
I dread going to work	2	1
I have low energy when I am at work.	2	1
I am having trouble sleeping	2	1
I seem to have little interest in my work lately.	2	1
I have feelings of emptiness	2	1
I experience physical aches and pains	2	1
I am easily irritated by co-workers or clients	2	1
I feel that my work lacks meaning.	2	1
I pull away emotionally from my colleagues	2	1
I believe that my work and contributions go unrecognized	2	1
I blame others for my part of a problem	2	1
I have considered quitting my job	2	1
I have a difficult time concentrating at work.	2	1
I am experiencing extreme fatigue	2	1
I am mentally exhausted at the end of the day	2	1
I lack excitement about my work.	2	1
I feel detached	2	1
I am quick to become angry	2	1
I am being cynical about my job and goals.	2	1

Job TOTAL = _____

Go to the next page for scoring assessment results, profile interpretation, and individual description.

Job Assessment

Scoring Directions and Profile Interpretations

The assessment you just completed measures your susceptibility to burnout from overworking. The items in the assessment are warning signs.

For each item on the previous page, count the scores you circled. Put that total on the line marked TOTAL at the end of the assessment. Then, transfer it to the space below:

Job TOTAL   =   _____

Assessment Profile Interpretation

If you circled even one TRUE answer, you might be at risk of burning out from overworking. The more TRUE answers you circled, the greater your risk of having a problem with an addiction to work. The HIGHER your score on the Job Assessment, the more of an issue you have due to work addiction.

Place an X on the line below for your score.

20 = Low	30 = Moderate	40 = High

How do you, or can you, walk the fine line between being a great employee and avoiding job burnout?

_____

_____

How worried are you about burning out because of working too much? What can you do about it?

_____

_____

If you have a work addiction or problem, it is best to consult a medical professional.

Non-Work Outlets

People with a work addiction fail to realize that they need non-work outlets because of the stress and pressure they put themselves under when working so much. They may not see the need for these outlets, but if left unchecked, the pressure can cause emotional problems, anger outbursts, and behavior that can harm their career and personal life.

Generally, physical activity is the best release for stress. *For example: martial arts, soccer, racquetball, swimming, bowling, bicycling, hiking, or simply walking a pet.* The way you release your aggression and stress is not important, as long as it's not harmful to yourself or others. What matters is that you find a way to let off steam.

Below, list some physical, non-work outlets that will allow you to let go of the pressure. You can write, doodle, or draw.

Letting off steam always produces more heat than light.
~ Neal A. Maxwell

I Will Say Yes!

To have non-work fun more often, start by saying "Yes!" People addicted to work often turn down invitations to get-togethers and say "No" when friends and family engage in leisure activities. Start saying "Yes" to more invitations that are not work-related.

You can make FUN a part of your life. Describe how you will say "YES" to things that are not work-related. USE NAME CODES.

I will say YES when _____ asks me to _____

_____

even though I _____

_____

I will say YES when _____ asks me to _____

_____

even though I _____

_____

I will say YES when _____ asks me to _____

_____

even though I _____

_____

I will say YES when _____ asks me to _____

_____

even though I _____

_____

In all of living, have much fun and laughter.
Life is to be enjoyed, not just endured.
~ Gordon B. Hinckley

Do Not Underestimate Sleep!

The amount of sleep a person has is important to provide balance when it comes to working hours and family time. Without enough rest, they will begin to deplete their store of energy, and the ability to think clearly becomes depressed. Without energy and clear thinking, they dramatically increase the chance of having too much work to do with too little energy to do it. It's a classic recipe for burnout.

For one week detail the number of hours per 24-hour day you sleep. Include sleep at night, as well as naps you take during the day. Before you begin documenting your sleep hours, guess the amount of sleep you are averaging per 24-hour day.

Hours_____

Days of the Week	Hours I Slept	Quality of My Sleep
Example: Monday	*8 to 8:45 pm – I took a nap when I came home and then had dinner.* *1 to 5 am – my night's sleep*	*Not very restful. I woke up several times at night thinking about a project due the next day.*
Monday		
Tuesday		
Wednesday		
Thursday		
Friday		
Saturday		
Sunday		

How can you begin to get more sleep?

_____

_____

Work and Life in Balance

For workaholics, work takes precedence over everything else in life. The desire to succeed pushes them to sacrifice personal well-being. Work-life balance is where people equally prioritize the demands of work and personal life. How can you maintain a better work and life balance by participating in activities you enjoy, caring about your loved ones and the concerns they may have, and developing better relationships with your family, friends, and co-workers?

Below, describe how you see yourself now and how you would like to be.

Work and Life Balance Themes	The Workaholic Person I Am Now	The Working Person I Want to Be
Example: Care About Yourself	*I now work over sixty hours per week and never take a vacation.*	*I want to work the regular work week and starting this summer I will use my vacation days.*
Care About Yourself		
Care About Loved Ones		
Develop Better Relationships with Family		
Develop Better Relationships with Friends		
Develop Better Relationships with Co-Workers		
Enjoy Yourself More		

It's all about quality of life and finding a happy
balance between work and friends and family.
~ Philip Green

Intellectual Wellness

Intellectual wellness involves exploring new intellectual activities, knowledge, skills, and creative abilities just for the fun of it. Enjoy new activities with family, friends, co-workers, etc., just for the pure enjoyment of it.

Below, draw or describe your intellectual self-image as you are now (skills, knowledge, creative abilities, activities) *and how you would like to be. Then list or draw activities you do now and fun activities you are willing to try* (learning a language, going to a museum, joining a book club, etc.).

Your Intellectual Self-Image	How You Would Like Your Intellectual Self-Image to Be in the Future
Activities You Do Now, Just for Fun	**New Activities You Could Try, Just for Fun**

Remember that whatever new activities and creative ventures you undertake, your natural tendency may be to be competitive. Try to do them just for fun instead of turning the activities into additional work and competition. Enjoy them!

Spiritual Wellness

Spiritual wellness includes cultivating meaning and purpose through activities, values, and relationships that support your wholeness. Most workaholics only experience meaning and purpose through their identity as a worker. They often do not take time to enjoy other life roles like parenting, being a great neighbor, or walking in the woods. They could join a group that practices yoga, meditation, worship, nature watching, bird identity, tai chi, etc. Spirituality allows you to find the inner calm and peace needed to get through whatever life brings.

Below, describe how you will begin integrating meaningful non-work activities into your life.

Meaningful Activities	How I Will Integrate Them	How It Will Increase My Spiritual Wellness
Example: Learn to meditate	*I would like to try to meditate before bedtime.*	*Meditation may help me clear thoughts of work before bed so I can sleep better and learn to value peace.*

I am deeply spiritual; I revel in those things that make for good – the things
that we can do to shed a little light, to help place an oft-dissonant universe back
in tune with itself... Long live art, long live friendship; long live the joy of life!
~ Jessye Norman

How can you find more meaning in your life that does not involve your job or work?

_____

_____

_____

Social Wellness

Social wellness involves building healthy, nurturing, and supportive relationships as well as experiencing a genuine connection with well-balanced people around you. Although you may work a lot that does not mean that you must push other people away or ignore them. Activities with family, friends, neighbors, etc., can be a great outlet to help you combat work stress. Positive social habits can help you build support systems and stay healthier mentally and physically.

Some Social Wellness Possibilities:
- Exercise with a buddy.
- Join a new club or organization that is not work-related.
- Make more friends outside of work so that you have some socializing to look forward to when you are not working.
- Plan a regular date night with your spouse or partner.
- Schedule a weekly movie night with your friends or family.
- Start a team or group (bowling, volleyball, etc.) to have fun in a social setting.
- Volunteer at a soup kitchen or other charity.

How will you increase your social wellness with family members?

_____

_____

_____

How will you increase your social wellness with friends or neighbors?

_____

_____

_____

To what charity can you volunteer to offer help and meet generous, caring people?

_____

_____

_____

What teams or groups could you join to have fun and enjoy yourself?

_____

_____

_____

Physical Wellness

Physical wellness involves an attitude that optimizes the effective and efficient functioning of the body. Physical wellness promotes care of the body for good health. It involves all of the items listed in the left column of the table below and quality time spent doing physical activities away from work with family and friends.

Think about how you manage your physical wellness lifestyle in each area below. Identify what you do now and what you would agree to start doing in the future.

Physical Wellness Areas	What I Currently Do	What I Will Start Doing
Drink Plenty of Water		
Eat Nutritionally		
Exercise		
Find Time for Fun		
Get Enough Sleep		
Manage Time Well		
Rest When Overworked		
Say NO to Unhealthy Substances		
Other		

What are the three most important physical things for you to do to prevent burnout, STARTING TODAY?

1. _____

2. _____

3. _____

Mindfulness

Mindfulness is the quality of being present and fully engaged with whatever you are experiencing at the moment, aware of your thoughts and feelings without getting caught up in them.

People addicted to work often live their lives on automatic pilot. That is not being mindful.

Read the following quote by Sylvia Boorstein and respond to the questions below.

Mindfulness is the aware, balanced acceptance of the present experience. It isn't more complicated than that. It is opening to or receiving the present moment, pleasant or unpleasant, just as it is, without either clinging to it or rejecting it.
~ Sylvia Boorstein

When you feel the need to work, what is going on in your body?

_____

_____

When you feel the need to work, what thoughts or emotions are you experiencing?

_____

_____

When you feel the need to work, are you present in the moment, or are you thinking about the past that is gone or the future that may never come? Explain.

_____

_____

When you feel the need to work, are you experiencing something pleasant or unpleasant in that moment? Explain.

_____

_____

When you feel the need to work, are you clinging to something or someone or rejecting something or someone? Explain.

_____

_____

© 2023 WHOLE PERSON ASSOCIATES, 101 WEST 2ND STREET, SUITE 203, DULUTH MN 55802 • 800-247-6789 • WHOLEPERSON.COM

SAY IT! "I Am Resilient."

Resilience is a skill that allows you to adapt to stressful situations such as overworking. It is the ability to recover from or adjust easily to misfortune or change and to bounce back.

On the line under each characteristic of being resilient, place an X on the continuum of how much you relate to the statement. On the dotted line below each one, write why you rated yourself that way. BE HONEST!

I adapt to overworking without lasting struggles.

| 0 (Not Much) | 5 (Somewhat) | 10 (Very Much) |

I have the skills to adapt well and recover quickly from overworking.

| 0 (Not Much) | 5 (Somewhat) | 10 (Very Much) |

I don't beat myself up about work-related failures.

| 0 (Not Much) | 5 (Somewhat) | 10 (Very Much) |

I have attainable work goals.

| 0 (Not Much) | 5 (Somewhat) | 10 (Very Much) |

I am aware of when I am working too much.

| 0 (Not Much) | 5 (Somewhat) | 10 (Very Much) |

I can bounce back when I get frustrated from overworking.

| 0 (Not Much) | 5 (Somewhat) | 10 (Very Much) |

HIGHER (Very Much) scores on each statement indicate that you are resilient.

MEDIUM (Somewhat) scores indicate that you are fairly resilient in these areas.

LOWER (Not Much) scores indicate that you are not very resilient in these areas and suggest that you need to be careful about your work addiction.

Keep a Positive Attitude

It is important to keep a positive attitude. This can be difficult when we are working way too many hours. We all experience times when things do not go our way or as expected. It can be challenging to remain optimistic when working long hours.

In the situations below, describe how you will become or remain optimistic.

Ways To Be Positive	Times I Become Negative	How I Can Be Positive
Example: Be around positive, fun people	*When I have been working many long-hour days in a row, I become grouchy.*	*Reach out to upbeat friends and ask them to take a long walk in the park with me.*
Be Around Positive Fun People		
See Value In Other People Even If They Don't Think as I Do		
Stay in the Present		
Control Only What I Can Control		
Do Not Make a Mountain Out of a Molehill		
Find Ways and Reasons to Laugh More Often		
Lend a Helping Hand to Someone in Need		
Put Myself in Another's Shoes to Appreciate My Own		

The high road and positivity is never the easy way but always the best way.
~ Nancy Wilson

How Do You Spend Your Energy?

Burnout is an accumulation of unmanaged stress from working too much and too hard, creating an imbalance between work and life. Working people may have **social obligations, leisure time activities, emotional wellness, intellectual pursuits, physical well-being, and spiritual nourishment** in their life in addition to their **work.**

Take a moment to look at your schedule or how you spend your time and energy. Are one or two categories above taking up most of your time and energy? For example, many workaholics spend as much as eighty percent of their energy on work, while the other people and things in their life receive very little attention.

In each circle below, identify a category and the percentage of energy you currently spend. Use the categories above, or add others that match your lifestyle better. The seven circles' percentages should add up to one hundred percent.

Next to each circle write the percentage of time you __intend__ to spend in each area.

To maintain a work-life balance, you need to make sure that all aspects of your life are receiving your attention.

© 2023 WHOLE PERSON ASSOCIATES, 101 WEST 2ND STREET, SUITE 203, DULUTH MN 55802 • 800-247-6789 • WHOLEPERSON.COM

Take Up a Cause

Although it is important not to over-schedule yourself, volunteering can contribute to a work-life balance. It can lower your levels of burnout and stress and boost your non-work self-esteem, emotional wellness, and social well-being.

What is a cause you care about? You could tutor, assist at a homeless kitchen or pet shelter, read to children in the library or at school, help the elderly in an assisted living facility, or help plan a community event. You will feel better about yourself and provide something to look forward to.

Write, draw, or doodle some potential places to volunteer your time.

Letting Go

Being overwhelmed and burned out is often the result of doing too much work and being too involved in other things. When this happens, it is time to look at your schedule and make conscious changes. If there is a work obligation or an activity that demands too much time and effort from you and doesn't give you what you need in return after putting in a great effort, perhaps it is time to let it go.

In the weekly schedule below, describe what you can let go of and how it will help you.

My Schedule	What I Could Drop	Ways It Would Make a Difference in My Life
Example: Saturday: My boss asked for volunteers to help organize the business on Saturdays. I said yes, and it's an all-day project.	*Some other people work there who have not helped. If we have a schedule where people come in for six weeks at a time, then others take their place, we could get the work done and not feel put upon.*	*I can spend time with my family during the day and go out for dinner with friends. I would look forward to it every day!*
Monday		
Tuesday		
Wednesday		
Thursday		
Friday		
Saturday		
Sunday		

The truth is, unless you let go, unless you forgive yourself, unless you forgive the situation, unless you realize that the situation is over, you cannot move forward.
~ Steve Maraboli

A Small Wellness Change

If you are a workaholic, you may be unable to make significant changes in your work schedule and life. Don't give up! It may be a slow process, but it can be done. Try making changes to achieve more balance in your life. For instance, set a goal to cut out junk food lunches at work and pack a healthy lunch to support your physical well-being. You can designate one night a week to spend with friends to increase your social wellness. You can spend an evening pursuing a mentally stimulating hobby or reading a book to improve your intellectual wellness.

Below, explore a small change you can make to have a more balanced, interesting life.

Wellness Areas	Examples of Possible Changes	Changes I Can Make
Emotional	Talk about my feelings about my work issues with my family.	
Intellectual	Take courses to improve my work status and not need to work so many hours.	
Spiritual	On my break, take a walk outside and notice the beauty, smells, sounds, etc.	
Social	Make plans with family and friends to do something together once a month.	
Physical	Find time to exercise a little bit every day, and then increase it.	
Mindfulness	Look around and be aware of the beauty and goodness around me.	
Optimism	Stay optimistic even when I am with very negative people.	

Wellness is the complete integration of body, mind, and spirit; the realization that everything we do, think, feel, and believe has an effect on our state of well-being.
~ Greg Anderson

Quotes about Maintaining Wellness

On the lines that follow each of the quotes, describe what the quote means to you and how it applies to maintaining wellness in your life.

Spiritual relationship is far more precious than physical.
Physical relationship divorced from spiritual is body without soul.
~ Mahatma Gandhi

_____

_____

Positivity attracts positivity.
~ Alyssa Edwards

_____

_____

My own path towards wellness has been a long and dynamic one.
It's taught me that healing from the inside out takes time and there can be great value in various sources of guidance.
~ Carre Otis

_____

_____

Wellness is not a "medical fix" but a way of living—a lifestyle sensitive and responsive to all the dimensions of body, mind, and spirit, an approach to life we each design to achieve our highest potential for well-being now and forever.
~ Greg Anderson

_____

_____

Which quote especially speaks to you about maintaining wellness? Why?

_____

_____

_____

_____

_____

Work-Life Balance

Name _____

Date _____

Work-Life Balance Assessment
Introduction and Directions

Work-Life balance is the lack of conflict between work and other life roles. It is the balance of demands on your personal life, professional life, and family life.

Work-life balance is a concept that describes the best way to split your time and energy between work and other important aspects of your life. When unable to achieve a work-life balance, people addicted to work will continue overworking and neglecting their other important life roles.

The following *Work-Life Balance Assessment* contains 20 statements that will help you to explore your current level of work-life balance.

Read each of the statements and decide if it describes you. If the statement describes you, circle the number in the YES column. If the statement does not describe you, circle the number in the NO column.

In the following example, the circled 2 indicates that the statement describes the person completing this assessment:

	YES	NO
When it comes to working behaviors:		
I over-commit at work	(2)	1
I unplug from technology to enhance personal time	(1)	2

This is not a test. Since there are no right or wrong answers, do not spend too much time thinking about your answers. Be sure to respond to every statement. The purpose of this assessment is for YOU to learn more about YOU and your work habits.

BE HONEST!

If you choose, no one else needs to see the results.

(Turn to the next page and begin.)

Work-Life Balance Assessment

Name _____ Date _____

This will only be accurate if you respond honestly. No one else needs to see this if you choose.

	YES	NO
When it comes to working behaviors:		
I over-commit at work	2	1
I unplug from technology to enhance personal time	1	2
I delegate some of my responsibilities if I can	1	2
I expect myself to be perfect	2	1
I make sure I have enough personal time	1	2
I spend as much time at home as I do at work	1	2
I am aware of the time I spend at work versus at home	1	2
I would rather be at work than at home	2	1
I am not happy unless I am working	2	1
I make home life a priority	1	2
I set boundaries so work does not spill into personal time	1	2
I take care of my health	1	2
I take on extra work no matter what is going on	2	1
I nurture my family relationships	1	2
I make time just for me	1	2
I leave work at work	1	2
I am unable to say "no" at work	2	1
I check work e-mails and phone calls even after work	2	1
I would work around the clock if I were asked to	2	1
I make time for relaxation	1	2

Work-Life Balance TOTAL = _____

Go to the next page for scoring assessment results, profile interpretation, and individual description.

Work-Life Balance Assessment

Scoring Directions and Profile Interpretations

The assessment you just completed is designed to measure the extent of your current work-life balance.

Add the numbers you circled on the assessment. Put that total on the line marked TOTAL at the bottom of the page. Then, transfer your total to the space below:

Work-Life Balance TOTAL   =   _____

Now place your score on the continuum line below.

_____
20 = Low   30 = Moderate   40 = High

Assessment Profile Interpretation

The HIGHER your score on the *Work-Life Balance Assessment*, the more of a work addiction you are experiencing. Circling even ONE number 2 answer indicates that you might be at risk of overworking. The more number 2 answers you circled, the greater your risk of experiencing issues because of a probable addiction to work.

Were you honest when completing the assessment? Is your score valid?

_____

_____

What is your reaction to your score?

_____

_____

How do you feel about doing something about your lack of work-life balance?

_____

_____

Time to Change Your Values?

If you are a workaholic, work is probably the most important thing in your life. Unless you truly believe that some other things or people are more valuable than work, it is unlikely that you will change your work-life balance. You won't be able to say "No" to overtime unless you sincerely say "Yes" to something you truly desire.

Prioritize the following things and people from 1 (Most Important) to 8 (Least Important). In the space under each rating, explain why you ranked the item as you did.

____**Work** *(job, tasks, responsibilities, etc.)*

_____
_____

____**Spare Time** *(hobbies, leisure, relaxation, etc.)*

_____
_____

____**Family** *(spouse/partner, parents, children, relatives, etc.)*

_____
_____

____**Friends** *(peers, people with whom you like to spend time, etc.)*

_____
_____

____**Community** *(neighbors, volunteering, etc.)*

_____
_____

____**Spirituality** *(mindfulness, religion, meditation, nature, etc.)*

_____
_____

____**Wellness** *(eating right, sleeping, self-care, exercise, etc.)*

_____
_____

____**Education** *(training, college courses, online learning, etc.)*

_____
_____

Re-Rank them in a way that reflects a better work-life balance:

___Work ___Spare Time ___Family ___Friends ___Community ___Spirituality ___Wellness ___Education

Who Makes it Possible?

Workaholics are so busy working that they often forget to appreciate the people in their lives who are affected by their work habits.

Think and write about non-work-related people you appreciate and how your work habits affect them.

People (USE NAME CODES)	Why I Appreciate This Person	How Does My Work Addiction Affect This Person
MKT	MKT is a great partner and an amazing parent to our children.	MKT works as well but needs to drop off and pick up kids, do the grocery shopping, help kids with homework, take them to appointments, friends, etc.

Have More Fun!

People addicted to their work rarely have time to just have fun.

Last week, how much time did you spend having fun, and what did you do?

_____

_____

_____

If you didn't have much fun, it's time to restructure your life a little. Let's explore ways to have fun outside of work.

- **What activities are exciting to look forward to?**_____

  _____

- **Who do you love spending time with?** _____

  _____

- **What new project can you get involved with that sounds like fun?** _____

  _____

- **What is something new that is a little risky but seems like fun?** _____

  _____

- **What is a new skill that sounds intriguing to learn?** _____

  _____

- **What can you do to get out of your comfort zone to have more fun?**_____

  _____

- **What are some ways to remain energized and motivated?**_____

  _____

I will start_____

I will hang out with_____

I will try something new like _____

I will get out of my comfort zone by _____

I will reconnect with_____

Do One Thing You Love to Do Every Day

Workaholics get absorbed into the flow of work-related tasks and responsibilities easily. They often forget to do non-work activities or to enjoy other people and activities that would bring them joy. One of the best ways to bring balance back into your life is to recommit to doing the things (other than work) that give you pleasure.

Think about the things you have always been passionate about, such as reading, jogging, watching a movie, meditating, playing an instrument, learning a new language, trying a new recipe, playing a card game, gardening, etc. Carve out time every day to do one thing that brings you joy. If you want to make it a new habit, do it daily for 30 days, and see how that feels. Journal about how you felt when you were done.

Days of the Week	One Thing I Did that I Loved	How I Felt Afterwards
Monday		
Tuesday		
Wednesday		
Thursday		
Friday		
Saturday		
Sunday		

Commit to doing one thing you love every day that you haven't done for a while. On the lines below, explain why you chose that activity.

_____

_____

_____

Schedule Me-Time

People who are addicted to work fail to recognize the importance of me-time. They fail to take time to relax and rejuvenate. Some ways to have me-time include taking a long bath, sitting outside, getting some exercise, and watching a great movie (all without working at the same time).

In each box below, write what sounds like great me-time. Next to each box, write how you can make it happen.

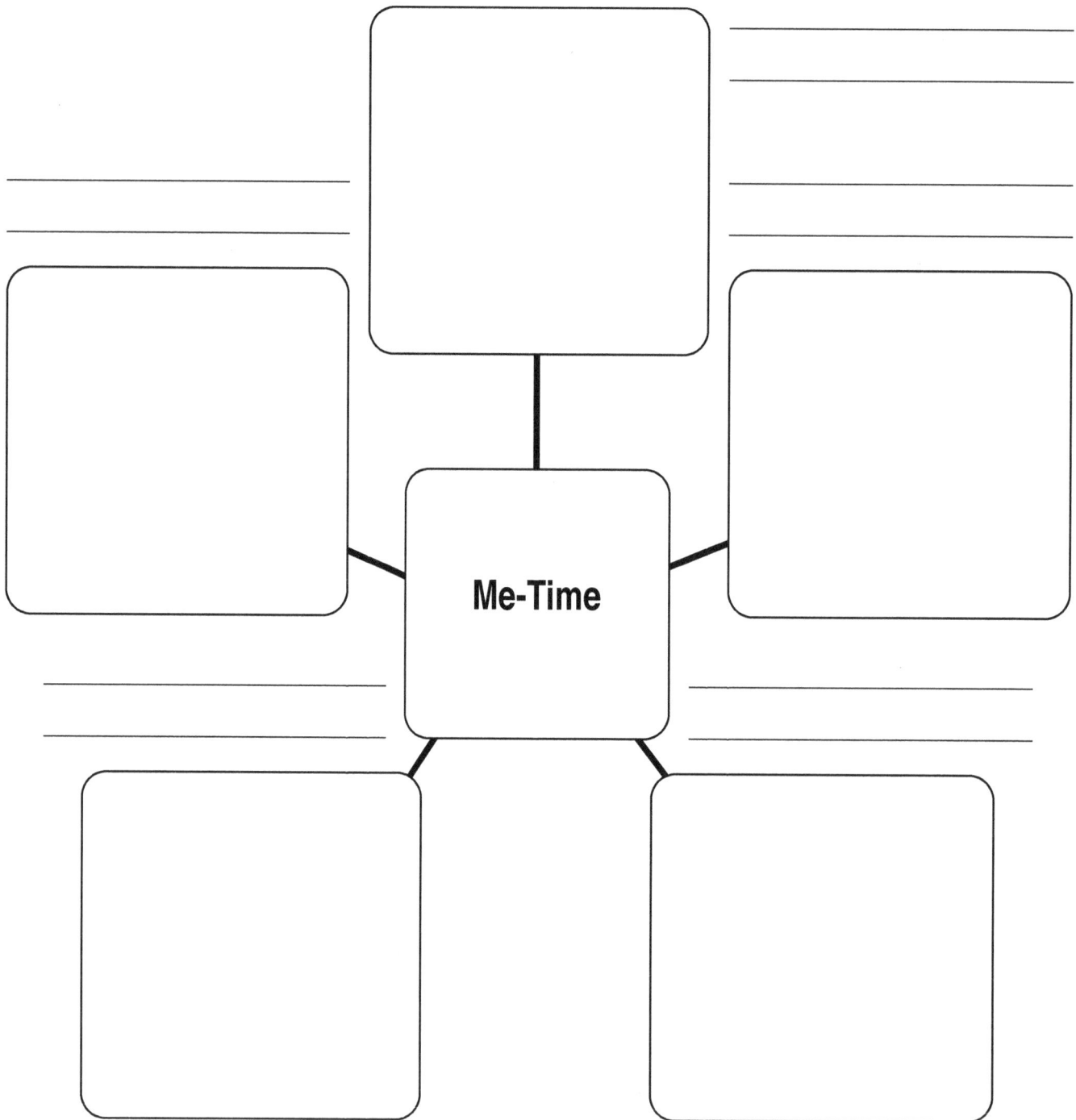

Me-Time

64000

Personal Goals

People who are workaholics set numerous goals for their work and their career. They set goals to succeed, make more money, and climb the career ladder. However, they rarely set goals for their personal life.

Setting goals for time with your family, friends, and spare time is important. These goals can include exercise, travel, hobbies, wellness issues, taking a class, volunteering, reading, cooking, etc.

Identify long-term goals (to achieve in a year) and short-term goals (to achieve in a week or two).

Non-Work Areas of My Life	Long-Term Goal	Short-Term Goals
Family		
Friends		
Wellness, Exercise, Sports		
Spare Time		
Religion, Spirituality		
Community		
Education		
Other		

Be More Efficient at Work

Workaholics make excuses for not getting their work done during work hours, so they must work late or take work home at night and on the weekends. Some ways workaholics could be more efficient: *keep distractions to a minimum, break tasks into smaller pieces, prioritize work, limit time spent talking on the phone, and delegate parts of the project to others.*

What are ways you can be more efficient at work? List them in the hexagons below.

Efficiency

Unplug from Technology

With technology to connect people at any time from virtually anywhere, there are few boundaries between work and home. The same technology that makes it easy for workers to do their jobs can absorb time with non-work activities *(gaming, texting, social media, shopping, etc.)*.

On the line under each characteristic of unplugging from technology, place an X on the continuum to show how much you think this statement describes you. On the dotted line below each one, write why you rated yourself that way. **BE HONEST!**

I limit the time I use technology for my personal life while at work.

0 (Not Much)   5 (Somewhat)   10 (Very Much)

I leave work at work and refuse to check technology after work.

0 (Not Much)   5 (Somewhat)   10 (Very Much)

I have established a time every evening when I check my emails.

0 (Not Much)   5 (Somewhat)   10 (Very Much)

I have reduced email access.

0 (Not Much)   5 (Somewhat)   10 (Very Much)

I prefer to have people rather than technology around after work.

0 (Not Much)   5 (Somewhat)   10 (Very Much)

VERY MUCH scores indicate that you are unplugging from technology.

SOMEWHAT scores suggest that you are sometimes unplugging, but not enough.

NOT MUCH scores indicate that you are not unplugging and that you need to be careful about allowing your use of technology to encourage your work addiction.

Establish Boundaries

Workers need to set appropriate and realistic boundaries for what they will and will not do at work and at home. This information must be communicated to your supervisor, coworkers, partner, and family.

Below, describe how you will establish boundaries between work and home.

Boundaries I Will Establish	How This Boundary Will Affect My Work-Life Balance
Example: I will commit to NOT working late on certain days unless there is a crisis.	*My family can count on me to be available on those days.*
Example: I will set aside time at home during which I will not check or respond to anything work related.	*I can watch a movie with my family or play a game without interruptions.*

We need to establish boundaries between our personal and professional lives.
When we don't, our work, our health, and our personal lives suffer.
~ Travis Bradberry

Unplug from Work Stereotypes

In addition to unplugging from technology, people with an addiction to work need to unplug from the stereotypes that honor overworking as a noble deed.

Following are some of the stereotypes of work. Write about what the stereotype means to you and how it affects the amount of work you do.

☐ Society encourages hard work. _____

_____

☐ Hard work will get you far in this world. _____

_____

☐ Hard work never hurts anyone. _____

_____

☐ Over-consumption and materialism are signs of success. _____

_____

☐ Competition is a good thing. _____

_____

☐ It is important to compare yourself to others and "keep up with the Joneses". _____

_____

☐ Abuse of power is to be expected by an employer. _____

_____

An employer has no business with a man's personality.
Employment is a specific contract calling for a specific performance....
Any attempt to go beyond that is usurpation. It is immoral as well as an illegal
intrusion of privacy. It is abuse of power. An employee owes no "loyalty," he owes
no "love" and no "attitudes" – he owes performance and nothing else.... The task
is not to change personality, but to enable a person to achieve and to perform.
~ Peter Drucker

Nurturing Relationships vs. Work

Workaholics often tend to ignore relationships while they are busy working. However, relationships with family, friends, and loved ones are a significant source of personal satisfaction. If your job or career damages your relationships, both areas will ultimately suffer. You need to ensure that your relationships become more of a priority.

Below, identify the people in your life and how to nurture a relationship with them.

People in My Life USE NAME CODES	The Status of Our Current Relationship	How I Will Nurture This Relationship
Example: GSP	*I have not been a very good friend.*	*I will spend more time with GSP and accept her invitation to a book club meeting.*

The relationships we have with people are extremely
important to success on and off the job.
~ Zig Ziglar

How are your relationships with people important to your work success?

_____

_____

Relax!

People addicted to work are often unable to relax. It is vital to find ways to unwind. Relaxing can help people rejuvenate from their work responsibilities, recharge, reduce stress, think more clearly, and make better decisions. Relaxation can include deep breathing, meditation, guided imagery, walking, reading, watching television, fishing, connecting to nature, writing down thoughts, making lists, and progressive muscle relaxation.

Below, write, draw, or doodle four ways you like to relax. If you do NOT take time to relax, write, draw or doodle four ways you would like to try to relax.

1	2
3	4

I love doing normal things—movies, shopping, going out with friends,
writing, reading, taking hot bubble baths—that's a big one for relaxation.
I also love to go to art and history museums.
~ Christina Aguilera

My Negative Self-Talk

If you work a lot, you might not notice that you have a stream of negative voices in your head that warn you about your job and work habits. This is called negative self-talk. These thoughts often fuel anxiety about work. Negative self-talk is something that almost everyone experiences from time to time, and it comes in many forms. It creates significant stress for us and, if we're not careful, for those around us.

Examples of negative work self-talk:
1. *"I can never get enough done."*
2. *"No matter what I do, my boss is never happy."*
3. *"I must work harder, or I will get fired."*

Examples of changing or reframing the above work self-talk positively:
1. *"I got a lot done. I'm happy with my performance."*
2. *"My boss thinks I can do more. I've scheduled a meeting to discuss goals."*
3. *"I know I am doing a good job."*

What is one of your usual negative work self-talk messages?

_____

_____

How can you reframe the above work self-talk message positively?

_____

_____

What is another one of your usual negative work self-talk messages?

_____

_____

How can you reframe the above work self-talk message positively?

_____

_____

What is one more of your usual negative work self-talk messages?

_____

_____

How can you reframe the above work self-talk message positively?

_____

_____

Prioritize Your Time

People who are addicted to work have long to-do lists. The problem is that when they prioritize their list, all the top priorities are work-related, not family-related.

If this is true for you, you must prioritize your work and home tasks into categories.

- Important activities have an outcome that leads to us achieving our goals, whether these are professional or personal.
- Urgent activities demand immediate attention and are often associated with achieving someone else's goals. They are often the ones we concentrate on and require attention because the consequences of not dealing with them are immediate.

Think about your upcoming week. Prioritize your personal (family, friends, home, etc.) and work tasks into the following four categories:

Urgent and important	Important but not urgent
Urgent but not important	Neither urgent nor important, but relaxing

How did you sort your activities for the week? What were the priorities?

_____

_____

Physical Activity Log (Page 1)

Workaholics often do not get enough physical activity. For one week, track the physical activity that you do during the week.

Physical Activity	Time Spent This Week On This Activity	How Did it Make Your Body Feel	How Did it Affect Your Attitude?
Exercise			
Ride a Bicycle			
Walk, Jog, or Walk a Pet			
Play Sports			
Work Out at a Gym			
Engage in Aerobic Activities			
Lift Weights			
Yoga, Tai Chi, etc.			

Physical Activity Log (Page 2)

Physical Activity	Time Spent This Week On This Activity	How Did it Make Your Body Feel	How Did it Affect Your Attitude?
Aerobics or Dance Classes			
Swim or Aquatic Exercise			
Physical Work Around the House			
Judo, Karate, Kickboxing			
Stretch			
Calisthenics			
Other			
Other			

Go back to the list and put a check by the activities you are willing to do more regularly.

Quotes about Work-Life Balance

On the lines that follow each of the quotes, describe how it speaks to your work-life balance.

Everything in life ... has to have balance.
~ Donna Karan

_____

_____

The more ways we have to connect, the more many of us seem desperate to unplug.
~ Pico Iyer

_____

_____

Life is all about balance. My work is very important to me,
but so are my relationships. I make time for that aspect of my life,
and it makes me happy having balance in my life.
~ Samantha Barks

_____

_____

When it is obvious that the goals cannot be reached,
don't adjust the goals, adjust the action steps.
~ Confucius

_____

_____

Describe what one of these quotes means to you and how it can apply to, or perhaps change, your life. If there is another quote that applies to you, explain.

_____

_____

_____

_____

_____

_____

© 2023 WHOLE PERSON ASSOCIATES, 101 WEST 2ND STREET, SUITE 203, DULUTH MN 55802 • 800-247-6789 • WHOLEPERSON.COM

WholePerson

Whole Person Associates is the leading publisher of training resources for professionals who empower people to create and maintain healthy lifestyles. Our creative resources will help you work effectively with your clients in the areas of stress management, wellness promotion, mental health, and life skills.

Please visit us at our website: **WholePerson.com**. You can check out our entire line of products, place an order, request our print catalog, and sign up for our monthly special notifications.

Whole Person Associates
800-247-6789
Books@WholePerson.com

www.ingramcontent.com/pod-product-compliance
Lightning Source LLC
Chambersburg PA
CBHW082359270326
41935CB00013B/1679

* 9 7 8 1 5 7 0 2 5 3 6 6 9 *